D1004157

Phyllis Shelton's

WORKSITE
Long-Term Care Insurance
TOOLBOX

Phyllis Shelton's WORKSITE Long Term Care Insurance TOOLBOX

Published by:

LTCi Publishing
108 Rhoades Lane
Hendersonville, TN 37075-8084
www.PhyllisShelton.com

This book is available at special quantity discounts for training, promotion and educational use by contacting the Publisher. For more information contact LTCi Publishing at 888-400-1118.

This book is designed to provide accurate and authoritative information in regard to the subject matter covered and is read with the understanding that the publisher and/or the author accept no responsibility or liability whatsoever with regard to errors or misinterpretation of the information contained within this book. Readers should not rely on this publication for legal or tax advice and should seek the services or a competent professional for such matters.

ISBN 978-0-9633516-8-5

Printed in the United States of America

Phyllis Shelton's

WORKSITE
Long-Term Care Insurance
TOOLBOX

DEDICATION

"Now unto Him who is able to do exceedingly abundantly above all than we ask or think according to the power that worketh in us."

—Ephesians 3:20

"Eye hath not seen and ear hath not heard nor entered into the heart of man the things which God has prepared for them that love Him."

—I Corinthians 2:9

There was never supposed to be a second book. My first book, **Long-Term Care: Your Financial Planning Guide,** *has been updated 15 times since it was first written in 1991, each time with much pain and suffering to me and all within 100 yards of me. I could never imagine contributing another literary effort of that magnitude to this industry. It's only appropriate to dedicate this book to its reason for being: the wind beneath my wings, my husband Bill, who would simply not let me rest until I promised to write it. Then I have to thank God, the real Author, Who empowered me to write it in a WEEK. The two verses above carried me through the entire experience and also through the Great Nashville Flood on May 8-9, 2010 as God delivered us beyond anything we could ask or think. I am also extremely grateful to everyone who encouraged and prayed for me throughout this effort and especially to Bob Bubnis, the only courageous layout artist who would even consider producing a book from start to finish in three weeks, and to Erika Liguori for her tireless efforts to design just the right cover.*

TABLE OF CONTENTS

Introduction

Some of you make so many trips to Lowes and Home Depot every weekend (or your spouse does) that they're probably making a reserved parking spot for you. The DIY Network with shows like *Kitchen Impossible* and *Flip That House,* or HGTV with shows like *Hammer Heads* and *Curb Appeal* have become mesmerizing television as the builders break down each step and make us think we can actually remodel our bathroom or kitchen ourselves. When you think about it, it's truly amazing how far the building trade has come for the do-it-selfers. A huge reason for that is because of all the great tools available but someone has to show us how to use them.

I want you to think of this book as your worksite LTCI toolbox and the best DIY show available for selling long-term care insurance through employer-sponsored programs. So when you see those flashlights throughout the book, you know to pay special attention!

I can't think of a better way to start this book than with a story that was emailed to me on March 30, 2010. It encompasses my strong feelings that people of all ages need long-term care insurance and this producer is spreading the word to the most fertile area to receive it – the worksite.

To: Phyllis@LTCconsultants.com
Subject: You jolted me into buying LTC insurance
      – thank you!!

I just increased the number of LTC insured's in the U.S. by 851 - and to think this all began with attending your training back in the mid-90's!

My husband and I were in our late 30's when I attended your training and quite frankly, you opened my eyes wide! I came home from your training and immediately purchased LTC insurance policies on myself and my husband. We have an only child who is now 24 yrs. old and I didn't want him to have both the financial and emotional burden of care for both of us. Three days after my husband's 45th birthday he had a grand-mal seizure at work - he was merchant marine and working off shore at the time - the diagnosis was a brain tumor. Anaplastic Astrocytoma Grade 3 - yikes! After surgery and 3 yrs. of radiation and chemotherapy treatment via MD Anderson Brain & Spine Center in Houston, TX, we are very happy to say that he is 8 yrs. tumor-free. We didn't have to claim any benefits from his LTC policy however, had I waited until we were older to purchase, I wouldn't have been able to buy it on him. As result, he is right-side impaired and has a speech impediment. He is also on a significant amount of seizure medication as that is the biggest struggle since the tumor diagnosis. He has some difficulty making decisions but he is indeed a brain tumor survivor - praise our LORD!

I do see some slight, gradual changes in his cognitive abilities over the last few years and just knowing that we have the LTC insurance gives me great peace. Me on the other hand, I think I'm just too ornery to peacefully die in my sleep at an early age. I feel my son is very fortunate that I have my policy so he can pay someone to take care of me - all I ask is that he come see me now and then!!

So, thank you, from deep in my heart, for your commitment and passion. I have settled in the large group market and have sold 17 new group LTC plans over the last 2 yrs. - the client average size is 15,000 employees with the largest one being 64,000 benefit eligible employees. My guess is that there are now over 10,000 recent LTC insureds through my efforts as a result of your training! My prayer is that one of my nursing home neighbors someday is an employee who chose to participate in one of these group plans!

Please feel free to share my story in your training sessions. It was great to personally meet you and I hope my story provides encouragement to further your commitment with great passion.

Kimberly A. Maginn
Austin, Texas

Since Kim focuses on the large group market for worksite LTCI, you will hear more from her in Chapter Nine of this book, *You Hooked Moby Dick – Now What?*

Ready to look through your new toolbox? Let's go!

CHAPTER ONE

WHY ARE WE HAVING THIS CONVERSATION?

Because the LTC insurance cheese has moved. It's that simple. For the last two years (2008-2009), about half of long-term care insurance sales have been made at the worksite.[1] And if you're not in that game, you simply can't get to the majority of the qualified prospects for long-term care insurance.

How did this happen?

We've had almost 20 years to sell the masses and spread the risk and we haven't done it.[2] There are about 7,200,000 million policies in force in the United States[3] versus:

- 113 million people over age 50
- 140 million over age 40
- 230 million people over age 18[4]

So whichever way you slice it, market penetration is still single digit. Not spreading the risk to the masses has resulted in:

1) the necessity to charge more for the product ; and

2) to be more selective about who can get it since the pool of

5

premium dollars with which to pay claims is much smaller than any of us thought it would be.

Hence, premiums are higher and underwriting is tighter. Decline rates are around 30% at age 65 and about 50% at age 75.[5] So it's no surprise that the average purchasing age has dropped to 56 in the individual market and 46 in the worksite market.[6]

But why should you care if you're selling long-term care insurance or not? Or if anyone else is for that matter?

Research from McKinsey & Co. finds that the average American family will face a savings gap of $250,000 at the time of retirement. Even with payments from Social Security and pensions, as well as personal savings in 401(k) and other retirement plans, the average family will have only about two-thirds of the income it will need. [7]

And Terry Savage, *Chicago Sun-Times* financial columnist devotes an entire chapter to "The Greatest Risk of All" in her book, **The New Savage Number: How Much Money Do You Need to Retire?**

What's the greatest risk in your financial plan? We've seen how a stock market crash can devastate retirement plans. But the greatest risk is not the longevity of this bear market, or even another bear market. It's the devastating cost of long-term care. And just as many pre-retirees didn't take the possibility of declining stock prices into consideration when making their retirement plans, most people don't consider the costs of living longer and the health-care and lifestyle implications. [8]

With quotes like these, how can anyone in any part of the financial services industry ignore long-term care insurance anymore? For that matter, how can any middle- and upper-income consumer believe that long-term care insurance is a luxury, not a necessity? Yet we see a single-digit market penetration for long-term care insurance staring into the face of 80 million baby boomers starting to turn 65 next year!

Having been in this market for 22 years, I do wish the objections would change – at least that would make it more interesting. Yet they stay the same.

As an industry, we've allowed people to tell us that:

- **they don't want long-term care insurance because they are never going to a nursing home -** instead of us telling them this can be the only thing that keeps people out of nursing homes by providing money to hire help at home; or
- **they are going to self-insure -** without input from us about the true cost of doing that by calculating care at future costs and the lost investment opportunity of pulling those funds out, particularly if it is bad time to do so; or
- **they're too young -** without us explaining they will pay more for coverage the longer they wait because they will have to buy a larger benefit due to inflation, and that there's a good chance they won't be able to qualify medically for a plan if they wait; or
- **they can't afford the premium because it is a bad economy -** instead of us telling them they simply cannot afford **not** to protect their retirement with LTCI.

As baby boomers transition from the accumulation phase to the distribution phase, advisors are in demand to construct an income stream that will last 20 or 30 years and even longer. Is there enough in the proverbial nest egg? Can a financial plan that guarantees one won't outlive her money be constructed for people who spend more years in retirement than they work?

The answer is ABSOLUTELY NOT – if the need to plan for long-term care is ignored. Let's take the gloves off. Do we care about our clients or not? Do we care about the person we see at the grocery store, sit next to at church, go to PTA meetings with? To ball games with? Our neighbors, our friends, and yes, our family? Are we talking about how essential it is to have this need taken care of in order to enjoy retirement? Because planning for an income to last 30 years means you don't want to have a bump in the road.

Here's a news flash. Long-term care isn't a bump in the road. It's an EARTHQUAKE. The resulting crater will swallow the best-laid retirement plan. Look how fast a couple can rip through $500,000 when only one of them needs care at today's cost of about $75,000 a year for 10 hours of home care![9]

Year	Assets at Start of Year	Income Needs	LTC Expense	Investment Yield	Assets at End of Year
1	$500,000	$60,000	$75,000	$30,000	$395,000
2	$395,000	$61,800	$78,800	$23,700	$278,000
3	$278,000	$63,700	$82,700	$16,700	$148,500
4	$148,500	$65,600	$86,700	$ 8,900	$ 5,000
5	$ 5,000	$ 67,500	$91,200	$ 300	($153,400)

Note: "Income Needs" is the portion of household income needs that the assets had been relied upon to provide and assumes annual inflation of 3%. "LTC Expense" is based on a typical annual cost and is subject to 5% annual inflation. "Investment Yield" is assumed at 6% annually after taxes.

However, in an economy similar to the one we have endured recently, we can change the investment yield to 4% and here is a more nearly accurate picture of how this could look:

8

Year	Assets at Start of Year	Income Needs	LTC Expense	Investment Yield	Assets at End of Year
1	$500,000	$60,000	$75,000	$20,000	$385,000
2	$385,000	$61,800	$78,800	$15,400	$259,800
3	$259,800	$63,700	$82,700	$10,400	$123,800
4	$123,800	$65,600	$86,900	$5,000	($23,700)
5	($23,700)	$67,500	$91,200	(0)	($182,400)

Oh, the client has $5 million dollars and can self-insure? Since when has any financial planner ever told a client with $5 million to forget about homeowner's insurance and pay full price for replacing a home? To pay full price for hospital and doctor bills? To pay full price for real estate, vehicles, art, jewelry, and whatever you do, be sure to pay top dollar for the new swimming pool?

However, I think there is a misconception about just how many Americans have several million dollars. The Financial Research Corporation says that less than 5% of households ages 45-74 have over $1 million.[10]

Are you starting to see how important it is to get to Americans with worksite long-term care insurance while they are young enough to afford the premium and healthy enough to pass underwriting?

And for those who do have a few million, I agree 100% with Harley Gordon, a founding member of the National Academy of Elder Law Attorneys, that long-term care insurance is really income protection, not asset protection. The person with $3,000,000 who plans to earn 5% in retirement income of $150,000 had better have a great plan if half of that income has to pay for caregivers starting next month, because he or she had a severe stroke. And what happens when the $3 million shrinks to $1.5 million as many have seen in the recent economic downtown? And if investment earnings shrink to 3%, not 5%? And the real clincher is if the 5%-6% growth rate over the last 20 years continues, long-term care costs will triple in the next 20 years.[11]   In 2030, we can be looking at over $200,000 a year, not $75,000 a year.

That growth rate can't continue, you say? I think something called the rule of supply and demand says it can. The demand for long-term care will be greater than ever in the history of the world with an aging population and in this country with 80 million baby boomers entering the care recipient years. The supply of caregivers is already at an all time low.

IT CAN'T POSSIBLY HAPPEN TO ME

When your client denies that anything will ever happen, try asking when the last time was that his nightly news station reported on a non-celebrity having a massive stroke? Not exactly news, since at least 700,000 people in the United States have a stroke every year, with one out of four being under age 65. [12]

> *My favorite cousin while I was growing up was Carolyn. I loved it when she baby sat me because she would show me her beautiful dance dresses. She had every color and was the best dancer I'd ever seen. Her brown eyes sparkled with happiness when she danced and she always had her most beautiful smile for me. She had a massive stroke at age 61 and has been paralyzed on the right side of her body and without speech for nine years. Her mind is fine. I know she remembers those dancing days.*

That means that most people need our help and *it's our job* to be sure they understand they need our help. Since when do we wait for people to walk up to us and say they need life insurance, disability income insurance or retirement planning services? The difference here is that long-term care insurance can be much easier to prospect for. Especially if you are a baby boomer, you will find that most of your peers are experiencing it with a family member and have learned the hard way that it isn't covered by anything else except Medicaid, which brings a plethora of limitations.

I continue to believe that long-term care is the REAL health care crisis in America and we only have a few years to get long-term care insurance to the masses in time to make a difference. This book is going to focus on the #1 way it can be done, and that is by selling policies to people at work while they are young enough to afford it and to be able to qualify medically. You know the old saying:

Money pays for the policy but HEALTH buys it.

Once a person has a severe progressive health condition like diabetes with complications, early Parkinson's disease, MS, multiple strokes and the like, no amount of money will buy a long-term care insurance policy in the individual market. This is almost true in the worksite LTCI market if it is simplified underwriting with a few health questions. These questions may not ask things like weight or hypertension or cholesterol, but it's becoming more common for simplified underwriting to require diabetes and stroke to be knockout questions – conditions that affect a significant percentage of the working population. Guaranteed issue is almost non-existent in the small group market, and that's where the action is.

Size matters. When we say that half of the long-term care insurance policies were bought at work, we are talking about a combination of true group and multi-life, but multi-life is driving the bus with a growth rate of 47% from 2007 to 2008.[13] Multi-life generally applies to the market below 100 employees and can extend up to 1,000. What exactly is multi-life, you say?

11

Multi-life LTCI is simply selling an individual long-term care insurance product to employees and their eligible family members with a premium discount and usually simplified underwriting. The simplified underwriting is a one-time opportunity when the plan is first offered and is truly a gift from the employer as many employees could never qualify for long-term care insurance in the individual market due to excessive weight or progressive health conditions. It is essential to emphasize this one-time opportunity heavily throughout the open enrollment period so that employees don't think they can get it next year or the year after as is the case with many employee benefits. Given that, you can see why hammering this point home is crucial for driving enrollment.

True group on the other hand may offer a one-time window for guaranteed acceptance. Why would you sell multi-life instead of a true group plan with guaranteed issue? As you will see in the rest of this book, there is some work involved with pulling off a really successful enrollment. Commissions are significantly smaller with true group and it can be really difficult to be adequately compensated for worksite LTCI sales with the typical true group commission level, especially if you have to pay enrollers or split with other producers. There are times when true group is the only way, especially if there are employees in a number of states as multi-life (i.e. individual) sales require you to be licensed and appointed with the carrier in all of those states. A true group plan only requires you to be licensed and appointed with the carrier in the state in which the home office is located.

The large cases are what I call whales and can take years to land at much expense. Moby Dick looks really great in the water but if you have a little boat, he can sink it in a hurry! So let's be clear. I'm not talking about knocking on doors of large employers and attempting to get them to implement large true group plans. But don't worry. If you develop a reputation for worksite LTCI, you will land a whale every now and then. We will talk about that in Chapter Nine *You Hooked Moby Dick – Now What?*

What I **AM** talking about is selling to small employers in your community with mostly voluntary LTCI using a multi-life chassis offered by many LTCI carriers. It's the way we can have the most impact on American families…in the shortest amount of time. Again, with 80 million baby boomers starting to turn 65 in 2011, we don't have much time!!

A multi-life long-term care insurance employee benefit offering is a win-win for all involved. **Families** win because they now have a viable solution for what I think is the real health care crisis in our country – long term care. **Employers** get to offer their employees a rich, new benefit that employees and their families are asking for and it doesn't have to cost the employer anything because it can be 100% voluntary. **Employees** save on their premium because they typically get a discounted group rate, many times with simplified underwriting. And finally, the **agent** wins because she/he is fairly compensated for the effort and typically gets full commission - just like on an individual LTCI sale - which is the way it should be because it is a significant amount of work.

IS IT WORTH IT?

You tell me. Are you sick of being turned down for individual long-term care insurance sales because of prospects complaining about being in a down economy and not having enough money to meet their every day cost of living needs?

13

Then the worksite LTCI market is for you. It's like switching from spinach to vanilla bean cheesecake with the yummiest graham cracker and walnut crust with chocolate and caramel drizzled over the whole thing. You can't get enough!

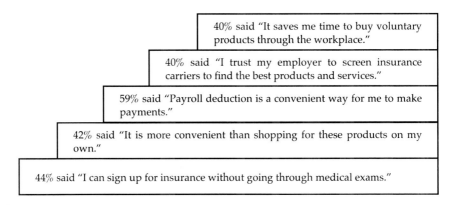

Since most employees are now going through LTC with a family member, they are hungry for the great news that there is a way to keep their own children from having to go through it with them. And amazingly, most employees aren't complaining about the economy. They are just appreciative that their employer cared enough to make LTCI available.

The MetLife 8th Annual Study of Employee Benefits Trends lists the top five advantages of voluntary benefits for employees. I smiled when I saw them because they mirror what I've seen in this space.[14]

40% said "It saves me time to buy voluntary products through the workplace."

40% said "I trust my employer to screen insurance carriers to find the best products and services."

59% said "Payroll deduction is a convenient way for me to make payments."

42% said "It is more convenient than shopping for these products on my own."

44% said "I can sign up for insurance without going through medical exams."

But the #1 comment we hear from employees is that they have been so worried about long-term care and were just waiting for their employer to do the shopping and offer them a reputable plan so they wouldn't have to go through the shopping process.

I've always believed that the fuse to the LTCI market is worksite. When I entered the long-term care insurance market in

1988 after 11 years of working with health insurance, it took me about three weeks to figure out that the market couldn't actuarially survive with selling just to people age 65+. The claims would be way too big to pay for people who had only paid premium for a few years. So I set my sights on a younger audience. Well, I'm not being entirely truthful with the reason I did that. The real reason was because of what happened when I was leaving one of my first seminars. I had used a hand-held microphone to deliver the seminar to the senior citizens' group at a Methodist church – 10:30, Monday morning.

Some of you are smiling already, I can feel it ☺

I was pushing open the door to leave when a precious white-haired lady tapped me on the shoulder to say "Honey, we really enjoyed your singing today!"

I do sing, but I wasn't singing that day. That was my wake-up call that the senior market would not be my footprint! I immediately established two essential requirements for any seminar audience from that day forward:

1) a broad mixture of ages (ages 40's and 50's were best); and

2) they had to have assets (homeless people can't buy anything).

After making that switch, I was very successful and enjoyed a much greater degree of job satisfaction because fewer people slept through my presentation. By early 1989, I was selling long-term care insurance to 40 year olds and averaging four sales a week, and hit ten one week! I would have sold to people under age 40, but that was the youngest most carriers would sell to in those days. I had one 39 year old woman who counted the days until her 40th birthday when she could buy, and she is still my client today. (One carrier at that time sold to all ages at about 50% less

15

premium for people under 65 and was out of the market in about four years.)

My background was group health insurance and I'm sure that played heavily into my certainty that worksite would be the fuse because it was the quickest way to get to younger, healthier people. UNUM published my first article containing that statement in 1991. But because of the rampant misconception that long-term care insurance is nursing home insurance for old folks, it has taken much longer than many of us ever thought it would to actually happen.

After enjoying significant success selling individual long-term care insurance to younger people in the early 90s, I began to get calls from producers all over the country asking me how I was doing that. My answer was simply that I educated them away from the objections and made them realize that this product is absolutely essential to preserve choices and dignity.

The reason I went into the long-term care insurance field in the first place was because I wanted to do something that would make a difference with my life. For those of you who don't know my personal long-term care story, I'll insert it here from my first book, **Long-Term Care: Your Financial Planning Guide**:

I was three when my grandparents moved in with us. My grandmother died unexpectedly two years later after gall bladder surgery. My grandfather was so sad. I still remember him crying after the funeral.

Born in 1886, my grandfather was blind, a diabetic who had to have a shot every day, and most importantly, my best friend. He listened with endless patience while I laboriously read the adventures of Nancy Drew, Cherry Ames, the Dana Girls, and Trixie Belden, none of which I ever finished. I think he also heard excerpts from Black Beauty and Beautiful Joe, my favorite animal books. Sometimes he returned the favor by telling me stories about his logging days in the East Tennessee mountains.

My mother was a nurse, worked nights while my father could be with us, and cared for my best friend almost ten years in our home, with my help of course. I didn't give him his daily insulin shot or plan his special diet or bathe him or dress him. But I gave him hours upon hours of my time, partially because I took the caregiving responsibility my mother assigned to me very seriously, but mostly because of how much I loved him. We had to be quiet while she slept, so I read him story upon story and fetched many glasses of water and led him to the bathroom when he asked me to. Sometimes I just crawled up on his lap to let him make whatever problem I encountered during the day go away. As I grew older, his room was my first stop when I got home from school.

My best friend went to a nursing home when I was 12. He never complained about anything or even asked for help, but I knew my mother was struggling between giving him her best (he was incontinent by then) and caring for me and my three-year-old brother. She was also working double shifts at the hospital for extra money. We moved him to another nursing home once because she didn't think he was getting the best possible care. When he passed away two years later, I was devastated. My best friend was gone.

Twenty years later, my mother lost a two-year battle with cancer at age 54. I thought about my best friend and finally realized that what was a normal lifestyle for me as a child must have been a tremendous sacrifice for her.[15]

Having been through this experience, it wasn't difficult for me to become an avid crusader for anything that would help a family at such a time. To this day I continue to say if there were a better way than insurance, I'd be on that bandwagon. But there just isn't.

Long-term care insurance is the most cost-effective way for family members to take care of each other when long-term care is needed.

When these calls from producers started coming in, I thought if I really wanted to make a difference with my life, I could write down everything I had learned and offer it to anyone so that producers could enjoy the same success I had anywhere in the country. The English major paid off and after creating a marketing system based on selling to individuals with an educational seminar or flipchart presentation, my consulting firm, *LTC Consultants,* was founded in 1991. To get my name out, I did one-day seminars in 23 cities in 1994 and about 1,000 agents attended these. This was not a profit-generating experience, but God is faithful. It broke even and all my needs were met.

The greatest thing that came out of this national tour was that carriers began to hire me to teach their agents how to sell long-term care insurance. After enjoying training contracts with ten of the top 15 LTCI carriers today and over 65,000 agents going through the training, I think the consulting and training idea was a hit. The main reason I think it worked well is because the producers in each class respected that I was teaching them what had actually worked for me. All these years, I've continued to sell – to family and friends mostly – but I kept selling to keep my training fresh so I would always know what is going on out on the street. I could see the worksite market coming, so I began pulling a worksite marketing system together in 2001, and wondered how I was going to test it so it would be as successful as my individual selling systems had been up to that time. I didn't have to wonder long.

In 2002, Moby Dick swam up to my boat when MetLife and John Hancock were awarded the Federal Long-Term Care Insurance Program (FLTCIP). MetLife asked me to deliver 1,000 employee education meetings to the Federal employees and after two weeks of solid deliberation, I invited him in. He almost sank our boat. After I verbally agreed to the job, the MetLife person said she was very glad to hear my decision but felt she should share that there had been a slight miscalculation and they now knew they would need 2000 meetings…in 4 ½ months. I think that is the longest I've ever stopped breathing. The program took on a life of its own and quickly grew from 26 cities to 210. It took 12 of our 13 employees plus 15 dedicated long-term care insurance producers that we recruited to provide the employee education for what evolved into the largest voluntary LTCI offering *ever* - the Federal government's LTCI offering to an estimated 20 million civilian employees, retirees, military, postal workers and their families.

We got the contract in March, and started the employee education meetings the first week of July. The 2000 meetings spilled over to 2020 that reached 88,449 federal attendees in 210 cities in 43 states. The 4 ½ months stretched to almost six to accommodate the additional meetings. Lots of juggling occurred as the carriers had to cancel a couple of hundred postal meetings and replace them with others.

One of the many learnings from that huge experience was that employee education meetings need to be at least 45 minutes and they must be on-the-clock. The postal service would only allow 30 minute meetings off-the-clock, so rather than do them for a handful of employees, LTCI Partners (the firm formed by MetLife and John Hancock to administer the Federal program) cancelled them and scheduled other meetings all over the country to use up the block of 2000 for which they had paid us. We were glad to accommodate but it challenged the careful regional representation we had orchestrated when we hired the 15 "Federal Navy Seals" as I called them, to undertake this daunting task. It all worked out though, and 269,000 people applied for coverage.

The drill-down on this for those of you who are really into stats is that the carriers could touch eight million people – half employees and half retirees. "Touch" meant either with mailings,

19

a video, a webinar, and/or all those meetings. The video consisted of the same information in the employee education presentation but in the form of a dialogue between a professional actress and me. The webinar (a brand new word to me at the time) was the presentation on the internet with my voice behind it. One million people raised their hand for information, 269,000 applied and about 202,000 policies were issued. The issue rate was lower than the application rate mainly because the coverage was not guaranteed acceptance. There were seven questions for employees, nine for spouses and full underwriting for all other qualified applicants. All in all, this initial enrollment effort was a huge learning experience for everyone involved and almost everyone was thrilled to be a part of it.

I say almost everyone because our Oklahoma City presenter quit after a week because we had to send him to Philadelphia right out of the box and I don't think he had ever seen traffic of that magnitude. He quit at 5:00 p.m. on Friday which was traumatizing for us because he was scheduled to do 24 postal meetings in Chicago that next week, starting at 8:00 on Monday morning. It was also unfortunate because I was scheduled to leave to do 29 meetings in Hawaii over the next two weeks and was scheduled to leave the next morning (Saturday) and couldn't make the switch to Chicago (did I say "wouldn't?") One of my employees who had been coaching the presenters through their presentations as we videotaped them to be sure they were perfect had made the mistake of working late that Friday evening. We immediately booked her a flight for Sunday afternoon and she found herself called up to the front lines to do those postal meetings with very little notice!

The Federal program resulted in three casualties in my firm including our VP of Operations, a former Naval officer (for real) who had been in charge of decommissioning a battle ship in three months during his tour of duty in the Navy. He said the Federal program made that project look like a picnic. (Don't worry, they didn't die – they just ran screaming into the woods at various points along the way. Our VP of Operations admirably stuck it out until the end but accepted a new position soon thereafter in a substance abuse treatment program (as a director, not a patient).

The Federal program was soon followed in early 2003 by a need for a firm to do the employee education for the 100,000 State of Tennessee employees and retirees. When the carrier that won that business asked if we could do 100 meetings throughout the state, we smiled happily and said we were more than up to the task. We didn't know until we read the next annual report that the enrollment was triple what the carrier had expected. In fact, the participation was 16% of the magic "40/40" group – the employees who were over age 40 with an annual income over $40,000.

By the end of that year, we were asked to help Blue Cross and Blue Shield of Tennessee offer long-term care insurance through their health insurance brokers throughout the state, so believe me when I say I've walked the walk and learned the worksite LTCI market the hard way. But even more importantly, for the purposes of this book, I've been personally involved in countless smaller enrollments, most of them from 10 – 500 employees but some larger ones as well all the way up to 5500 employees. Once again, I was thrilled to have this experience as I desperately needed a laboratory to test my ideas for successful worksite LTCI enrollments.

There is nothing like real case studies to prove a point. So here are three actual worksite enrollment results from cases I personally worked on while test marketing my worksite enrollment system. Read the results carefully because there is a dramatic difference between industry averages and these actual results. I think you'll understand the reasons why by the end of this book.

Worksite Case Study #1:

Small regional bank - 97 employees

Actual voluntary enrollment results:

80 Applications (38 employees, 23 spouses, 19 family members)

Employee Participation = 39% (not including spouses and family members)

Industry Average Participation 4 - 5 %

Total Number of Applications vs. Number of Employees = 82%

Estimated Commission if only industry average participation was achieved = $1,655 ($600 average premium)

Actual 1st year commission on this case: $26,488

Worksite Case Study #2:

Insurance Company statewide office - 927 employees

Actual voluntary enrollment results:

404 Applications (233 employees, 140 spouses, 31 family members)

Employee Participation = 25% (not including spouses and family members)

Industry Average Participation 4 ½ %

Total Number of Applications vs. Number of Employees = 44%

Estimated Commission if only industry average participation was achieved = $15,180 ($900 average premium)

Actual 1st year commission on this case: $122,016

Worksite Case Study #3:

Medical College - 1016 employees

Voluntary enrollment results:

131 Applications (107 employees, 21 spouses, 3 family members)

Employee Participation = 11%

Industry Average Participation 4 ½ %

Total Number of Applications vs. Number of Employees = 13%

Estimated Commission if only industry average participation was achieved = $35,399 ($1,300 average premium)

Actual 1st year commission on this case: $90,927

Now I know these results might sound exaggerated, but they're not – they are REAL! According to one respected industry consultant, the industry average participation in voluntary worksite LTCI is an abysmal 4-5%.[16] If I collectively compare the three case study results with the industry average, this would be the result:

- Estimated Commission if only industry average participation was achieved = $52,234
- Actual 1st year commission on these three cases: $239,431

The process I follow is always the same - whether it is a small or large group. It all starts with **education, education, education.** In my opinion, too many agents/brokers get the employer to say YES to a voluntary enrollment, then go in and do an employee seminar and expect above-average participation. I say the results are directly related to the educational effort. If you don't want industry-average voluntary enrollment, don't follow standard

23

industry worksite enrollment practices. The worksite process I follow and teach is the result of years of fine-tuning and as many of you have heard me say over and over about my individual sales training:

"If you do it exactly the way I teach it to you, you will succeed in spite of yourself!"

Ok – let's get started. I'm going to make this really easy for you, and we will start with baby steps.

CHAPTER TWO

YOU CAN'T BUILD A HOUSE WITHOUT A PLAN

It's fascinating to me that America's Health Insurance Plans (AHIP, formerly Health Insurance Association of America) in Washington DC said in 2007 that **57% of people over 50 report they've never been approached to buy long-term care insurance.**[16]

Then at the March 2010 Intercompany Long-Term Care Insurance Conference, we heard that 57% of employers have never been approached to offer long-term care insurance to their employees.[17] Coincidence?

Who knows…but with the single-digit market penetration that we discussed in Chapter One, the only way is up, right? One thing's for sure - I know we can do a better job as an industry reaching out to qualified prospects, whether they be individual or part of an employee group. The best news of all is there's never been a better time or more needed time to talk about planning for long-term care.

But first, we need a plan.

Just how big is the worksite LTCI market?

The Bureau of Labor Statistics 2008 National Compensation Survey reports 150 million employees in the nation. The number of employees with access to long-term care insurance has more than doubled since 1999 from 6% to 14%. However, that breaks down to only 6% in firms with less than 100 employees and 24% for 100+ employee firms. [18]

There are 6 million firms in the United States and 5.9 million of them have less than 100 employees. [19]

Less than three million long-term care insurance policies have been sold through employer-sponsored programs, whether true group or multi-life. [20]

The number of workers in the 55 years and older age group is projected to grow by 43 percent by 2018, over five times the 8.2 percent growth projected for the labor force overall. This group is projected to increase by 12 million and make up nearly one-quarter of the labor force in 2018. [21] Why is this significant? Because this age group represents the prime caregiving years. Most will wind up becoming caregivers for spouses or aging family members, but some will become care recipients with early long-term care events brought about by strokes, Lou Gehrig's disease, early Parkinson's or Alzheimer's, and the like.

Back to the plan. Although the 55+ age group is growing faster than any other segment of the workforce, don't make the mistake of focusing just on employers with predominantly older employees. While a firm with all 20-somethings won't be your best target, the idea is to get long-term care insurance in front of a broad mixture of ages, just like you want to do in the individual market. You might be surprised at how many people in their 50's can't qualify for long-term care insurance, which plays a role in why the average worksite LTCI purchaser is 46. [22]

Thanks to growing consumer awareness efforts about the need to plan for long-term care, we're finally starting to see a time in which a wider age group of employees is aware of it. What are those efforts and when did they start?

1) **2002: The Federal Long-Term Care Insurance Program.** When the largest employer group in the world started offering long-term care insurance as an employee benefit, a strong message was sent to the private sector about its importance.

2) **2006: The Long-Term Care Partnership.** The Deficit Reduction Act of 2005 which was signed into law on February 8, 2006 made it possible for all states to implement a partnership between long-term care insurance and Medicaid. Policyholders who buy a tax-qualified policy with the correct inflation benefit for their application age group are allowed to shelter one dollar of assets for each dollar of benefits paid out when they apply for Medicaid. Most states don't require the policy benefits to be exhausted before people can apply for Medicaid. This means that people can apply for Medicaid at whatever point they become unable to make up the difference between the policy benefit and the cost of care at claim time. Accordingly, some states limit the amount of protected assets to the benefits paid out as of the date of Medicaid eligibility while others allow the amount to grow even after one is on Medicaid. Either way, Medicaid pays AFTER the long-term care insurance benefit has paid, which saves the Medicaid program (and the state taxpayers) a significant amount of money.

Does it work? It's a home run! Four states have had Partnerships since the early 90s (Connecticut, New York, Indiana and California) and out of around 312,000 policies, only 369 policyholders have had to turn to Medicaid for help after using their long-term care insurance benefits.[23]

3) **2006: The *Own Your Future* program.** The Deficit Reduction Act allocated $3 million per year through 2010 for states to conduct

a consumer awareness program on the importance of planning for long-term care with help from the federal government. At a minimum, the program is kicked off with a press release from the governor and a mailing to everyone in a 20 year age band (usually 45-65) inviting respondents to ask for a brochure and CD. The #1 method of planning for long-term care mentioned in the educational material is long-term care insurance. The response rate for the program has been upwards of 10% and as of early 2010, this outreach has happened in 24 states plus the District of Columbia (Arkansas, Colorado, Georgia, Idaho, Iowa, Kansas, Kentucky, Louisiana, Maryland, Michigan, Missouri, Nebraska, Nevada, North Dakota, New Jersey, Ohio, Oklahoma, Pennsylvania, Rhode Island, South Dakota, Tennessee, Texas, Virginia, and Washington). Unfortunately the government won't release the names of the people who asked for information but you can go to www.longtermcare.gov and order a copy of the educational materials if you don't already have them. There is a brochure you can hand out which is very powerful since it has been distributed by your state in conjunction with the federal government. (Good news - the new health care reform bill included $15 million over a five year period to continue these education efforts.)

4) **About 2006: Long-term care insurance carrier national advertising really started happening.** Bankers Life, Genworth, John Hancock, Mutual of Omaha are some well-known carriers that have paid for national television advertising. They are to be commended as this outreach goes **a long way** to making long-term care insurance more well-known and accepted.

While these statewide and national awareness campaigns help, it's up to you to reach out to the employers in your community.

There are many ways to get in the door of the small employer and it doesn't have to be by cold calling. And you don't have to buy a list and start massive mailings either. The best entry point is to simply network with other insurance professionals and let them open the doors for you. Sometimes you split the commission and other times you don't have to.

One of the most successful ways to break into the LTCI worksite market is to network primarily with other insurance professionals who are employee benefit specialists, as they already have access to the group market. Just as is the case when you network with other professionals in the individual market, these group benefit specialists must trust that you won't infringe on any of the other products they have in place with each employer. They are typically very busy selling an assortment of products and don't have time to specialize in long-term care insurance. A relationship with them is a win-win. You can make them look good by enabling them to bring a much-needed benefit to their group clients, and they can get you a warm welcome that you may not otherwise be able to get with some accounts.

In addition to networking with employee benefit specialists, don't overlook the networking opportunities that you normally pursue in the individual LTCI market. Civic groups, Chamber of Commerce related functions, professional organizations related to specific occupations are all fertile ground for uncovering interested worksite prospects as small business owners and benefit managers are frequently members. Networking with other professionals in your community such as the provider community (directors of home health agencies, nursing homes, assisted living facilities and adult day care centers) as well as centers of influence such as accountants, attorneys, owners of investment firms, bank officers, etc. frequently turn up leads.

When you become the "go to" person in your community for long-term care insurance, prospects will call you. (My High-Impact Seminar Selling System has a roadmap for how to accomplish this.)

When they call, be sure to discover if the caller is a prospect for worksite LTCI while you are asking the normal pre-qualifying questions about health, assets and decision makers. (My High-Impact One-On-One Selling System contains this list of questions.)

If the caller is a business owner, ask if the company is a C-corporation. If so, you can simply say, "Great, *(Mr. or Ms. Benefit Decision maker)*! Do you realize that as a business owner you have access to a worksite long-term care insurance plan with premium discounts and underwriting concessions and that the entire premium is 100% tax deductible for you, your spouse and your dependents? And although many plans are 100% employee paid, any premium that you contribute for your employees is also fully tax deductible as a business expense?" Sound extremely excited as you explain this information.

A natural objection at this point in the conversation is there is no money for a new employee benefit. Quickly assure the business owner that many plans are 100% employee paid and it won't cost anything but a payroll deduction slot and access to the employees to do the employee education. The business owner/decision maker doesn't even have to offer it to all employees, but he or she can benefit from the group discount and modified underwriting if a group plan is offered and a minimum of *(insert the participation minimum of the carrier(s) you represent)* employees purchase a policy. Emphasize that the IRS allows the employer to select by class so the business owner can allow the company to pay his or her premium and deduct it as a business expense (if the company is a C-corporation), and that it doesn't require the same offering for all employees. Don't dwell on why it would be good to contribute to the premium at this point. Save that for the benefit manager presentation when you describe long-term care insurance in Chapter Five, *The Blueprint of the Perfect Employer Sales Presentation.*

An agent in Kingsport, Tennessee, used this language with an existing client to sell a 10-pay with full return of premium: "*(Name of client)*, if I could show you how to take approximately $150,000 out of the company for a personal benefit for you and *(client's wife)*, with the blessing of the IRS and then pass it all on to your children after the last death of you and your wife, regardless of any benefits paid, would that be of interest to you?" She then went on to explain that at age 55, this plan could be fully funded by age 65 when he retires, relieving him of the burden of budgeting for premiums after retirement, and in this case, she illustrated a 10-pay with return of premium at death, regardless of claims.

Think of how many worksite opportunities there could be if you work with 3-4 health insurance brokers in your area! Or you could go in with any number of agents who have worksite accounts and specialize in other products - but not LTC insurance. Worksite LTCI prospects are everywhere – the people you know at church, in civic groups, in parents and teachers organization, in almost any type of social setting. However, it has been my experience that most business owners/decision makers are loyal to the benefits brokers they already work with, so approaching those brokers will be a much easier path for you.

So your plan? Simple. Identify a good working list of employee benefits brokers in your community. Join organizations like the National Association of Health Insurance Agents and other professional organizations to meet them. Find out about any type of broker training for group benefits sponsored by health insurance carriers in your state, such as Blue Cross Blue Shield. Have plenty of business cards to hand out at these events and if you really want to attract attention, put a tag line on your business card that says something like: *helping employee benefits specialists offer worksite long-term care insurance.*

You can also join local employee benefits organizations. The Society of Human Resource Managers (www.shrm.org) is a national organization with local chapters that you can join.

With any of these contacts, be on the lookout for another wonderful source of worksite long-term care insurance referrals: the employee benefits consultant. Many of these organizations are fee-based and are not allowed to accept commissions for their work. Employers are asking them more and more frequently for advice on offering worksite long-term care insurance and sometimes to conduct a Request for Proposal (RFP) process. When you can become to go-to person in your community for worksite long-term care insurance, you can become the first person these consulting firms turn to when an employer brings up the subject of long-term care insurance. But rather than wait for that to happen, you should be proactive and call on as many of these firms as possible to let them know you are in this business.

A wonderful side benefit to doing all of this networking is that you will receive speaking invitations to the local chapters, and that is a home run! The employer presentation as outlined in Chapter Five, *The Blueprint of the Perfect Employer Sales Presentation* is a perfect presentation for these events. Normally that presentation ends with asking the employer to offer long-term care insurance. You would change that ending to one that allows the companies to indicate they want a no-obligation consultation with you about a long-term care insurance worksite offering. You will use a response form just like you would in a consumer seminar, except it will be tailored to an employee benefits professional audience. You can have a place on the response form for the benefits decision maker to indicate the employee benefits specialist he or she works with so that person will be included in the appointment.

HOW DO YOU GET THE REFERRAL?

That's the main question, right? Well, it's the same technique that you use when you are cultivating centers of influence like accountants, attorneys, financial planners, etc. for individual referrals. You have to do an educational presentation but many of these professionals will brush that off and say they already know everything about long-term care insurance. So to get around that, you tell them you will only feel comfortable working together if you have the opportunity to show them the educational presentation that you will do for their clients. Guess what? Getting worksite LTCI referrals works exactly the same way. You simply make an appointment with targeted employee benefit professionals and offer to do the employer presentation so they can see what you would do for their corporate clients. Notice I said "targeted". You only want to work with those who do business with the type of corporate client that makes a good prospect for worksite LTCI. You will learn more about that in the next chapter, *Prospecting: Beef Stew or Flattened Squirrels?*

WHAT ABOUT COMMISSION SPLITS?

If you haven't been around the world of health insurance for awhile, you may not know that group health insurance commissions are usually well under ten percent in the under 100 employee range and perhaps 3% in the 100+ employee range. One successful health insurance broker told me he sees about $250 in annual revenue per employee. This can be much less than long-term care insurance commissions, even when they are split, so you are offering these brokers a chance to increase their revenue significantly with very little work on their part.

Some long-term care insurance specialists use the Million Dollar Round Table (MDRT) commission split table which is designed to reflect how much work is actually done:

20% for the lead
20% for the appointment
20% for the benefit design
20% for closing the sale
20% for ongoing service

I think it is difficult to adapt this model to worksite LTCI because as you will see in the upcoming chapters, there is a significant amount of work for you to do throughout the enrollment process. Accordingly, other LTCI specialists I know always do a 50/50 split and leave it at that so there is never an argument.

There are a couple of considerations, however. If the health insurance broker contracts under you and you are going to get an override on that business, you can easily do a 50/50 split and come out fine. If the broker is under someone else and doesn't do anything other than take you into the account, then it is reasonable to do 70/30 and I know some who go as far as 80/20. If the health insurance broker is under another MGA, you can ask the insurance company about a "dual appointment" which means you can split across hierarchies with no problem. You want to be able to split on the application however you work it out so the renewals come to you seamlessly and you or the health insurance broker aren't relying on each other for commission payments.

To give you a more clear idea of how this works, let's use $1,000 premium. The carrier usually splits that premium based on the percentage you and the health insurance broker have decided to use, then pays each of you at your respective commission levels with that carrier. For example, a 50/50 split would look like this:

Health insurance broker: $500 premium x 60% commission level = $300
You: $500 premium with a 70% commission level = $350

It is normal for you to have a higher commission level as you write more LTCI volume than the typical benefits broker would sell. If the health insurance broker is writing under you, your override would be on top of your share of the broker commission. On a 70/30 split with you doing all the work, your share of the broker commission would look like this:

Health insurance broker: $300 premium x 60% commission level = $180
You: $700 premium with a 70% commission level = $490

Either way, LTC insurance can offer an employee benefits broker a significant income stream for just getting you into the account and supporting your efforts to make the sale with the employer.

And if you really want to make it easy for this to happen, you will give all of your referral sources a brief, door-opener presentation they can use to get the employer to meet with you and listen to the entire benefit manager sales presentation. The door-opener presentation is outlined in Chapter Ten of this book, *Are You a Rainmaker or a Builder?*

It's easy to get caught up in a shotgun approach but in summary, **cultivating employee benefit brokers and consultants is the richest source of leads for worksite LTC insurance.**

Jed's baby picture

CHAPTER THREE

PROSPECTING: BEEF STEW OR FLATTENED SQUIRRELS?

There's a little black lab at our house named Jed Clampett, whom we affectionately refer to as our Tennessee mini-lab. We rescued him from the woods in which his mother had taught him to survive. Left to his own devices, he would earn his Tennessee namesake's reputation almost daily because he loves to hunt, and he is very good at it. He is lightening fast and sneaks up on his prey like a stealth bomber. The little bunny or baby squirrel never knew what hit 'em. Since we are all animal lovers around our place, that had to stop and it stopped pretty much the day we put a bell on Mr. Jed. Now the baby animals in the forest can hear him and scamper quickly away when he goes into his stalking mode.

But before we took such drastic action, Jed was bringing home "presents" and the stinkier, the better. His favorite seemed to be the flattened squirrel. Sometimes I think it was roadkill and he was just cleaning up the environment by bringing it home to his human family. Whatever he brought, he was so proud and would drop it on our front deck with a flourish, expecting the utmost praise.

Why am I regaling you with this tale? Because just as in any other insurance sale, there are good prospects and poor prospects. Just as with individual long-term care insurance sales, you will find it necessary to train the referral sources that you develop for worksite LTCI as to what a good prospect is for long-term care insurance.

Ideally a prospect will satisfy the 40/40/40 rule: at least 40% of the employees are over age 40, have an income of $40,000+ and at least 40% are female. The income will vary based on geographic region. With high-cost areas, $40,000 is too low and you might even make that threshold more like $75,000 or more. Even in middle America, it's becoming the norm to want 40% of the employees to have incomes in excess of $50,000, not $40,000, for two reasons:

1) inflation – the cost of living is much higher today than when the 40/40 rule was originally set up a decade ago; and

2) premiums have increased significantly in the long-term care insurance market, especially in the younger ages. Between 2006 and 2008, I saw premium for a 40 year old couple increase about 22% when I did my annual premium comparison of about ten carriers.

Five developments are driving the higher premiums:

1. **longer life spans** which make the 5% compound no max inflation benefit very scary to price when the average purchasing age in worksite LTCI is only 46. A guaranteed acceptance plan is really frightening to carriers as employees become more educated and finally understand what a gift that is, especially as it relates to the 5% compound no max inflation benefit;

2. **lower than anticipated lapse rates:** In the early stages of long-term care insurance, I heard an expected lapse rate of 15% thrown around. The lapse rate today could be better referred to as a death rate since it is well under 2%;

3. **lower than anticipated earnings on reserves:** Rates set with an expectation of earning 7% on reserves are not going to be sufficient any way you look at it if earnings fall to 3%;

4. **better claims information:** As long-term care insurance has been around in a meaningful form now for at least 20 years, the actuaries have a better idea about benefit utilization and behavior and are able to use pricing methods other than the dartboard approach; and

5. **NAIC regulation** back in 2000 laid out stiff penalties for any carrier practicing an inappropriate pricing pattern. These are on pp. 90-91 in my book **Long-Term Care: Your Financial Planning Guide** but I'm going to insert them here so you can develop a higher level of confidence in today's long-term care insurance rates. I have found that it helps employers to be aware of this list of penalties as well so they are able to better trust the pricing of today's carriers. Most states have passed it:

- The 60/40 loss ratio requirement for long-term care insurance, which means that at least 60 cents of every premium dollar must go for benefits, is eliminated. The NAIC thinks that's an incentive for rate increases - the higher the rate, the more money the other 40% generates for administrative costs.

- Rates must be actuarially certified that they aren't expected to increase ever under moderate economic conditions.

- When a rate increase is approved by the state, 85 cents of each rate increase dollar must go to benefits and only 15 cents can go to administrative costs.

- The applicant must sign that he or she understands rates can increase. *(This is part of the personal worksheet in today's applications.)*

- The insurance company has to disclose at time of sale the rate increase history on similar policies for the last ten years. *(This is part of the personal worksheet in today's applications.)*

- If a rate increase is approved by the state then turns out to be unjustified, the insurance company has to refund the money to the policyholders.

- If an insurance company exhibits a pattern of inappropriate rates, the insurance commissioner can prevent the company from doing business in that state for five years.

In addition to these rate increase deterrents, this regulation also requires carriers to include a contingent non-forfeiture benefit at no additional premium. This just means in a nutshell that a policyholder receives a nonforfeiture benefit, even though he didn't pay extra for it if his premium goes up past a certain predetermined point based on issue age. The age-based table with the corresponding rate increase percentage trigger is in each long-term care insurance product's Outline of Coverage and the actual policy if your state has passed this.

For example, the rate increase trigger point is 70 percent for someone who purchased a policy at age 60, and the 70 percent trigger point is cumulative. If the insured had three rate increases and the third one took the premium to 71 percent more than the original premium, the insurance company would have to give that person a nonforfeiture benefit that is equal to a "shortened benefit period".

This means the insured could stop paying premium and the insurance company would have to pay a claim at any point in the future equal to the premium the person had paid in. Hence, the name "shortened benefit period" as benefits will be paid at the current daily benefit but only as long as possible until all the premium paid into the policy has been returned in the form of benefits. Or, if the insured wanted to keep the policy in force without the additional rate increase, he or she could do so by accepting a reduced benefit offer that the insurance company is required to extend at that time. The daily benefit might be lowered, for example, but the insured could keep the same premium without accepting that last rate increase that would have sent the premium past the rate increase trigger point.

This type of nonforfeiture benefit can be purchased with additional premium when the policy is first purchased but most people don't buy it. The NAIC wants all insurance companies to provide nonforfeiture contingent on future rate increases. Because they believe insurance companies don't want to give this benefit away without the additional premium it normally costs, the NAIC thinks this will be an incentive for the insurance companies to do everything possible to hold the premium down so it won't increase to the point that makes the company provide this nonforfeiture benefit free. (Again, if you want to provide this information to prospects, it's all in Chapter Two, *Features of a Good LTCI Policy* of my consumer book **Long-Term Care: Your Financial Planning Guide.**)

The female percentage recommendation is a little more complex. Since two-thirds of caregivers are women, at first glance you might think the higher the female percentage, the better. [24] Not so. My experience has been that if the female percentage is too high, you run into the "I have to ask my husband" objection much more frequently. Some of this is mitigated by the type of position women hold within the organization. If we're talking about a high percentage of managerial women, I'm not as concerned as these women are decision makers or they wouldn't be in those positions. Decisive women who really care about their families do drive the sale.

Probably the most touching example of this I've heard recently came from one of my own clients, Mr. C. Vernon Duckett. He and his wife Helen bought long-term care insurance policies from me back in 1990. He called out of the blue one day and demanded as soon as

41

I answered the phone, "How in the world did you talk me and my wife into buying these long-term care insurance policies?" Fearing that this would be my first complaint from one of our policyholders in the 20+ years I've been in the long-term care insurance field, I carefully answered, "Well, Mr. Duckett, your wife Helen invited me over to talk to you and then you bought – why, is there a problem?" His reply elicited a quick sigh of relief on my part, then tears as I listened while he assured me it was the best financial decision he had ever made in his life. It turned out his wife Helen was in a nursing home with Alzheimer's. He tearfully told me that his wife Helen was his most precious asset, not his money, and the fact that the long-term care insurance policy he had on her enabled him to give her the best care possible meant more to him than anything at that point. At my request, he wrote me this beautiful letter:

To: Phyllis Shelton
From: C. Vernon Duckett

*I enjoyed talking with you the other day about how we met and how Helen and I made the decision to buy an LTC policy. So you know money was tight in those days. I want you to know that we will be **eternally** indebted to you. Just think you were interested in us enough to call when you knew of a better policy that had Life Time Coverage with a 5% Rider good until age 86. This has turned out to be the best investment we ever made. This LTC policy has given me peace of mind, security, and independence. As you know, I have had two heart attacks, and it's great to be able to go to bed at night and know that my precious wife will be taken care of the rest of her life. I know that the Lord had His hand in this all along.*

Thanks again,
C. Vernon Duckett

This story won a Lifetime Foundation award and appeared in the September 14, 2009 issue of *Newsweek*. If you want to show a

4 minute video of this very moving story to your clients, you are welcome to do so by using this link:

http://www.ltcconsultants.com/articles/2009/clientstory/storyvideo.shtml

So let's take a close look at my list of attributes that make for a really good long-term care insurance prospect.

CHARACTERISTICS OF A GOOD WORKSITE LTCI PROSPECT

Contrary to popular belief, there are many wonderful group prospects other than groups of doctors and attorneys and similar white collar professionals. Here's a checklist you can use when evaluating groups for long-term care insurance:

- Does the owner feel paternalistic toward the employees and take care of them accordingly? (Or "maternalistic" as one woman-owned conglomerate quickly corrected me.)
- Does the employer value the employees and consider turnover expensive?
- Do most of the employees have long tenure and seem loyal to the employer?
- Does the employer try to tie employees to the company with benefits?
- Is the company stable; i.e. no mergers, acquisitions, layoffs?
- Does the company already offer a great benefit package, including voluntary benefits?
- Is there good participation in the other voluntary benefits?
- Are many of the employees "planners" who are concerned about taking care of their families and planning for a successful retirement? **MOST IMPORTANT BUYER CHARACTERISTIC!**
- Do many of the employees have some college education? *(most LTCI purchasers have some education beyond high school)*

43

- Is the average age of the group 40 or older?
- Is there a significant number; i.e. 40%, of employees with an annual salary of $40,000 or more? *(Customize for your area.)*
- Are at least 40% of the employees female? *(Women tend to drive the sale but be careful – if the female percentage is too high, you run out of women who are decision makers and the "I have to check with my husband" objection takes over.)*
- Last but not least, it's not a good idea to offer long-term care insurance immediately after a health insurance rate increase. (See Chapter Twelve, *The Blooper Chapter*)

If I had to pick one characteristic over the others, it would have to be whether or not the employees are planners. Are they buying lottery tickets on their way to work as a retirement planning tool while refusing to invest in the 401(k)? Does "mutual fund" mean we're all having a lot of fun? (Let's all thank Jeff Foxworthy for a bit of humor with this definition.)

If they are investing in their retirement fund with pre-tax dollars regularly plus participating in other voluntary products, you've got yourself a great worksite LTCI prospect.

My second favorite characteristic is education. Generally, if employees are doing retirement planning, they are more highly educated than the general population and that's how they understand the need to plan.

I've already mentioned this point in the first chapter but it bears repeating: A really refreshing aspect of the worksite LTCI market is that with qualified groups with employees who are educated and planners, you rarely hear complaints about the economy. Just the opposite, these employees understand the need to plan for long-term care. Their focus is more on understanding the true cost of long-term care and understanding how fast the cost of care is growing and becoming a very serious threat to their financial plan to not outlive their income.

Back to Jed Clampett. What type of prospect would I consider a flattened squirrel in this market? Here's a partial list and I think you will quickly get the idea:

- Uneducated – municipalities (city and county employees) can fall into this category as well as retail and service industries.

- An average age younger than 40 as you will typically attract a lot of young families. In a group with broader ages, many of these younger employees will enroll, but I'm convinced that is helped by some mentoring coming from the older employees who truly understand the importance of the long-term care insurance benefit in general and of the underwriting break in particular

- An average salary less than $40,000

- Companies with the bulk of the employees not having access to email or regular communication channels.

Public schools for K-12 are challenging because these teachers have lower salaries, are younger and often in more entry-level teaching jobs, and the communication system can be much less efficient than in private schools or private industry.

Hospitals are especially challenging as it is so difficult to communicate with the employees who can afford long-term care insurance such as the nurses and staff physicians and other professionals.

However, just because a group isn't a good prospect for a voluntary benefit offering to all employees, doesn't mean you can't approach it to do an offering to the owners and executives.

Therefore, don't overlook asking every business owner you meet about long-term care insurance if you think he or she is health and financially qualified, because tax incentives for long-term care insurance are better for business owners than for individuals.

Owners of C-Corporations can deduct 100% of the premium for the owner and spouse, including a 10-pay, and self-employed business owners can deduct an age-based amount that usually increases each January based on medical CPI. Here's a snapshot of LTCI tax incentives for employers to offer long-term care insurance to have under your belt:

- Premiums for employees, spouses and dependents are a tax-deductible business expense to employers just like health insurance.
- Premium contributions are not taxable income to employees.
- Benefits up to $290 a day ($8,800 per month) are tax free to employees and beyond as long as the benefit doesn't exceed the cost of qualified care. (This is an advantage LTC insurance has over disability income insurance.)
- Employers can select by class (tenure, salary, job title) for an employer contribution or for the offering itself.
- An age-based amount of long-term care insurance premium can be paid with pre-tax dollars through a Health Savings Account.

Long-term care insurance is an especially effective way to reward key executives. Since premiums are treated like health insurance and are therefore 100% tax deductible for employees and spouses (including owners of the corporation for a C-Corp), the tax deductibility extends to a "10-pay plan" – a plan that is paid up in ten years.

If you need to brush up on the tax incentives for long-term care insurance, see Appendix A. You also don't want to forget any state tax incentive for long-term care insurance. A quick reference chart for those can be found at the Kaiser Family Foundation website at this link:

http://www.statehealthfacts.org/comparetable.jsp?ind=381&cat=7&sort=a&gsa=2

CHAPTER FOUR

WHO IS THE DECISION MAKER? OR IT'S NOT ABOUT YOU (MS. OR MR. HR PERSON)

While we're on the subject of prospecting, I have to warn you about something I've learned the hard way. The HR person usually isn't the best place to start when you approach an employer about offering long-term care insurance.

Surprised? I was. I thought a Human Resources Director was this warm, fuzzy Mrs. Doubtfire or Andy Griffith type person who nurtures all of the employees and looks out for their best interest 24 hours a day. And every now and then, the HR person actually fits that mold. But not usually. More often than not, the HR director is someone who is over-regulated to the max and has to deal with a veritable buffet of benefits all the way from the essential medical insurance plan which is always in a state of upheaval to pet insurance. My most tear-jerker caregiver story doesn't phase them because they simply don't have time to listen. Ouch. My feelings are crushed and I take this brushoff very personally. Am I toast in this situation?

No, because I've learned not to start with that person. The last thing in the world many of the HR directors want to hear about is a new benefit offering and especially one that we want offered apart from the annual benefit fair. After a few of those "You want it WHEN?" looks, I knew this can't be the right person to talk to.

This is a really broad problem because if you are networking with a health insurance broker, the HR person may be the only management level person the broker has a relationship with. So as you form these relationships, you have to carefully search out the level of decision maker your referral source actually has access to.

Depending on the size of the company, you need to start with the owner, the president or Chief Financial Officer. At the very least, start with the Vice President of HR, not the HR Director. When we cover the essential elements of the employer presentation in Chapter Five, you will see why. Much of the conversation centers around long-term care insurance being "Productivity Insurance" which means it will lower things like the absenteeism rate and requests for part-time assignments or even resignations. The people who care about these things are the people who run the company...the people who are conscious of the bottom line. The idea is to get that person's attention, have that person (or persons) make the decision to offer long-term care insurance, then have that person bring in the HR Director as the implementer, not the decision maker. Otherwise, the HR Director can quickly turn into the Terminator as he or she torpedoes the worksite long-term care insurance sale.

Why would they do that? Because a new benefit offering means more WORK and they are already so overworked!

Don't get me wrong. There ARE wonderful Human Resource Directors in the universe. My top two are in my all-time hall of fame as thoughtful, diligent professionals who care about their employees, and will do anything I ask to get employees to appreciate the incredible benefit offering of long-term care insurance. Both of these individuals didn't have an HR background when I encountered them. One had actually been a consultant to small businesses. When her husband accepted the position of head of the business school at a private college, the college president was so impressed with her that he offered her the job of HR Director.

The other HR person was a pharmaceutical distributor before accepting the job of HR Director.

Both of these individuals continued to send out notices to the employees about the open enrollment period and personal consultations with no prompting from me...because they cared and knew it was the right thing to do.

So when you are networking with your referral source, you need to ask a lot of questions about the person(s) the referral source knows at the company:

1. job title
2. decisionmaking position in the organization
3. how has this person handled other benefit offerings – did that person make the decision or someone else in the organization?
4. how does the person feel about the employees? Do you sense that maternalistic/paternalistic attitude or is the HR position just a job ?

Your time is precious. Be very diligent about pre-qualifying your referral sources. You want sources who can get you into the decision makers. It's better to have three or four solid referral sources who can do that vs. ten health insurance brokers who work only with an HR person who just handles the day-to-day administration of the employee benefits.

CHAPTER FIVE

THE BLUEPRINT OF THE PERFECT EMPLOYER SALES PRESENTATION

Those of you with background in the individual long-term care insurance market know that the first question out of your mouth at any appointment is "Have you had a personal experience with long-term care?" I had to modify that question over the years because many times, people would shake their heads "no", then be telling me in the next few minutes about how long their mother had to take care of their dad at home. Because of the hard-to-break connotation of the phrase "long-term care" with "nursing home care", it's better to ask:

"Have you had anyone in your family who has needed home care for several months or longer? Or anyone who has needed care in an assisted living facility or a nursing facility?"

Then you will collect a lot more "yes" answers. You naturally follow with questions about what caused the need for care, how it was paid for, and how it affected the lifestyle of the primary caregiver(s).

Well, guess what? You don't deviate from that when you are in front of the employer prospect. Find out where the decision makers are in their own personal experiences with long-term care. That puts them into the zone of those feelings and will make them more receptive to your presentation.

Have you noticed I continue to refer to a presentation? There are several successful ways to sell long-term care insurance, with the two most popular being what I refer to as the "trial attorney" method and the educational presentation. The trial attorney method involves asking a series of questions which "leads the witness" into believing it's a good decision to buy long-term care insurance. This is a very effective way to sell long-term care insurance but you have to be a master at it. To become a master at it, you normally become an apprentice of someone who is a master, and the learning curve can take several months. And if you are not a master at it, you can get yourself off track, get your client off track, and ultimately talk yourself out of a sale. You can see how that process makes it difficult to teach that method to the masses.

The method that has worked for me so successfully over the years is the educational presentation method. I tried the "send a letter and call people for an appointment" method like so many of us and failed miserably. Well, I only made three phone calls but that was enough for me to call it a failure.

The first person who answered the phone was unintelligible, incoherent, and I couldn't understand one word. (I found out later that my company had sent letters out to age 65 and up, with no age limit so this person was probably 95 years old!)

The second person who answered the phone was not as thrilled to hear from me as I had been led to believe by my enthusiastic sales manager.

The third person couldn't have been nicer. My hopes rose as he thanked me for calling like I had made his day. He then kindly explained that he didn't need my services that day because he already had someone to mow his yard.

Lawn care. Be there – 1988.

I dumped the list of names and phone numbers unceremoniously on my young manager's desk at that point and was on my way out the door when he said, "Wait – why don't you try the seminar presentation?" My ears perked up because I was used to giving presentations in my previous health insurance life. I've already explained earlier in this book how quickly I found out that senior seminars were not for me, but once I started doing seminars for people with a broad mixture of ages and assets, life got much better and I was on my way to a long, successful career in long-term care insurance. There were two additional milestones along the way, however, that might help you to know as they also apply to worksite LTCI sales.

One, I used a response form after the seminar which I always called an evaluation form with my audience. I told them I needed their comments about my presentation so I could learn and improve it as much as possible. After the "what did you like and what didn't you like" questions, the last question asked "do you want more information about long-term care insurance?" I found that most people checked "yes" to the last question about wanting more information just to be nice.

When I called them for an appointment, most of them weren't serious.

Soon, I was doing a lot of seminars with very few sales. I knew enough to call them quickly as the forms weren't like wine – they definitely didn't get better with age, but it didn't help. Most people didn't want an appointment. Out of desperation when I had enough of the forms to wallpaper my living room and no way to know who was serious about wanting my help and who wasn't, I told my next audience that the question about wanting more information really meant "do you want to see me for a no-obligation consultation to customize a plan for you?" I went on to be brutally honest and told them if they didn't check "yes" to that question, I would never call them. This takeaway close worked extremely well and people seemed to appreciate my honesty. I still had to pre-qualify them when I called for health and financial suitability, but I wound up getting appointments with many more qualified prospects. The point here is that when you do seminars for groups of employer decision makers, always use a response form, call it an evaluation form, and end the seminar with a similar question:

"If you would like a no-obligation consultation to determine if long-term care insurance is an appropriate benefit to offer to your employees, please check "yes" to the last question on the evaluation form; otherwise I won't call you."

The second turning point was reached when I began to get referrals from people who had not attended a seminar. I would get so excited about the appointment, explain the product information and wind up back in my car with blank applications. After a few of these, my young manager redeemed himself again from those awful cold calls by suggesting that since they hadn't heard the information in the seminar, they couldn't make a buying decision. Off we went to the office supply store, and he bought me a white markboard, four colored markers and an aluminum easel. I would take all that into people's houses, explaining as I entered that they were lucky I didn't bring my slide projector and big screen, set it up and draw the same presentation I did in the seminar. I drew it a screen at a time, using the four different colors for emphasis...drew and erased, drew and erased. Now my handwriting is almost illegible, but I think the fact that they saw the information as well as heard it allowed them to absorb it much faster and reach a buying decision much more quickly. And one more thing. Since I hate objections so much, I built them into my presentation so that I was addressing all of their objections before I offered to help them with their application.

In short, I've never sold a long-term care insurance policy just in a conversation. Today, I get referrals and wind up helping people over the telephone, but I still go through a mini-presentation to be sure they understand the main points before we go into the plan design phase.

Now that you've heard this background, you will understand why it came natural to me to develop an educational presentation for employers and employees to help both reach a decision to buy long-term care insurance. I'm not saying any other method of selling long-term care insurance is wrong, because it isn't. I'm just saying I can only teach you what works for me.

In worksite LTCI, there are two levels of selling.

First, you must convince the employer to not only offer it but to understand its importance enough to allow you to do the proper employee education.

Second, you have to convince the employees to buy long-term care insurance, no matter what age they are.

This chapter will look at the first level, convincing the employer. There are three parts:

1) Clearing up the basic misconceptions about long-term care

2) Explaining to the employer why it is so important to offer long-term care insurance (includes the tax incentives)

3) Explaining the plan itself (how to get a claim paid, who is eligible, features and benefits, sample premiums, how to enroll and the employee communication plan)

PART ONE: CLEARING UP THE MYTHS

The first advice is the same as I've given in my individual long-term care insurance training sessions all these years. Don't ever assume your audience knows the basic components of long-term care. I was in health insurance for eleven years and didn't understand them. So whether you are meeting with the smartest attorney, accountant, bank trust officer, financial planner or in this case, employee benefit consulting firm or the actual employer decision makers, chances are, the person or persons hearing your story do not understand the basic points that make long-term care insurance a necessity, not a luxury.

Combining these basic points with a seminar style that includes some validating quotes from national authorities works well to get an employer's attention to the subject. After the quotes, you can go into these basic points:

1. Most long-term care doesn't happen in a nursing home; in fact, most people will never be in a nursing home as less than 15% of LTC happens there[25]

2. Long-term care happens to people of all ages (over 40% of people who need care are under age 65)[26]

3. Long-term care is expensive ($75,000 a year for a 10 hour shift of home care or care in a nursing facility—*adjust this to your area*) and expected to triple in the next 20 years[27]

4. Health insurance and Medicare don't pay for long-term care as they only pay for short-term, recovery care as long as the patient is showing progress, so typically for less than three months.

5. Most long-term care is paid out of pocket or by Medicaid, the state/federal welfare program that pays after one has spent down most resources[28] (*Optional statement here if you are offering a Partnership plan:* "…unless you buy a special state-approved long-term care insurance policy that allows the policyholder to protect assets equal to the benefits paid out before turning to Medicaid for help")

6. The odds of needing care are high, greater than one in two at age 65[29], much higher than other risks we routinely insure like automobiles and houses.

7. Summary: Long-term care is very expensive, very likely to happen and not paid by anything else until you have spent most of your resources, and has a devastating impact on the family.

PART TWO: WHY SHOULD THE EMPLOYER OFFER LTCI?

Once these decision makers understand what long-term care actually is and that anyone of any age can need it, you can explain these two crucial elements:

1) the impact of long-term care on the productivity level of the employer's workforce; and

2) the devastating impact of long-term care on a family.

Hence, long-term care insurance is "Productivity Insurance" for the employer because:

- A **tidal wave** of caregiving is about to hit U.S. employers as the fastest growing part of the workforce is the age 55+ employees who are in the prime caregiving years[30]
- The impact of caregiving on productivity will be **HUGE**:
  a) workday interruptions to handle medical visits and phone calls

b) increased absenteeism and leaves from work

c) decreased motivation and morale

d) increased ongoing stress which can eventually lead to health problems for the caregiver which ultimately leads to more health insurance claims and higher health insurance premium – the last thing employers want!

e) decisions to ask for part-time work or resign altogether which increases replacement costs

- Two-third of caregivers are women, and women make up 47% of the workforce, [31, 32] so this caregiving tidal wave could be the greatest threat to everything women have accomplished in the workplace!

- Caregivers whose family members have long-term care insurance are TWICE AS LIKELY to stay in the workforce as those whose family members don't have it[33]

And long-term care insurance is "Lifestyle Insurance" for the employee because:

- Your employees have worked hard to get to where they are in life. Many have dreams beyond the workplace – vacations, travel, a specific college choice for their children.

- A spouse or parent having a stroke or accident can torpedo those dreams and take your employee off your payroll in the blink of an eye.

- Being able to afford paid caregivers in that situation can make all the difference by

  ⇒ giving your employees the peace of mind to know their loved one is being taken care of while they are at work;

  ⇒ providing the priceless advantage of preserving the quality of relationships between siblings; e.g. by reducing arguments over who will be the primary caregiver; and

  ⇒ preserving the role of a daughter or son instead of turning them into personal caregivers providing help with personal tasks such as bathing, dressing and toileting which most of us don't want our adult children doing for us anyway.

- The financial assistance of long-term care insurance frees up money for college educations and retirement savings instead of having to spend it on caregiving.

The greatest benefit of long-term care insurance to employees is to REDUCE STRESS, both by helping with future caregiving needs when their family members have purchased it and by not having to worry about their needs being taken care if they or their spouse need long-term care at a younger age.

You will want to round out the "need" part of the employer presentation with a statement that the government is encouraging long-term care insurance with tax incentives for employers to offer long-term care insurance, plus the Federal government has been offering it to the Federal employees since 2002. (See p. 46 in Chapter Three for a summary and Appendix A for the detail.) If there are questions about the CLASS Act from the national health care reform, you can just say:

"The health care reform law includes a very small benefit for long-term care that is mostly dependent on payroll deduction but employers are not required to offer it and employees can opt out. The main concern is that the premium will cost much more than anticipated."

You can see Appendix B for a more detailed description and a sample handout to employers or employees if you need one.

If you offering a Partnership plan, you can let your employer prospect know that your state government is also encouraging long-term care insurance by offering asset protection for those who buy long-term care insurance in the event they ever have to turn to the state Medicaid program for help with long-term care.

PART THREE: HOW DOES LTC INSURANCE WORK?

I like to start this section with explaining how a claim is paid, as that is where the rubber hits the road about this insurance in my opinion. I'm always very concerned that consumers will think this is short-term care insurance. So I go out of my way on this part to be sure they understand it isn't a broken leg or even a broken hip. With today's technology, expecting to need help at least three months represents a severely limiting situation. I also always say that benefit access is controlled by Federal legislation, in order to get the tax incentives of long-term care insurance, including tax free benefits. That way no one thinks insurance companies can define it differently. I also use some humor on the cognitive portion of the explanation as this subject can get depressing in a hurry and this is a good place to lighten the mood. I point to the slide that shows the six activities of daily living and say:

"You can qualify for benefits either physically or mentally. Physically means a health care practitioner - which means a doctor, registered nurse or licensed social worker - has to let the insurance company know that you are expected to need help with at least two of these basic six activities of daily living for at least 90 days. So it isn't a broken leg or even a broken hip with today's technology. It could be a bad accident in which you broke both your legs and your hip and wound up needing help 6-8 months with bathing and dressing and getting around, or it could be a severe stroke that causes you to need help for an extended period of time. If it's cognitive, it has to be severe enough that you are a threat to yourself or someone else. If you can't remember to take medicine for high blood pressure, for example, you could cause yourself to have a stroke which makes you a threat to yourself. If you will walk out in the middle of the interstate, you could be a threat to 20 other people. Do you understand?"

WHO IS ELIGIBLE?

It seems to be a well-kept secret that long-term care insurance is open to so many family members in addition to the spouse or partner: (I think we need a new term for this – how about "spartner"?)

Parents
Grandparents
Siblings
Adult children 18+

I usually say if we included cousins it would take in the rest of the state but you probably won't want to include that in your presentations outside of Tennessee. ☺

On a serious note, I ask if anyone has 20-something children whom they would be responsible for if that child were involved in an accident. I know of two situations in which that very thing happened and I cite them. Both were automobile accidents. One was the son of one of my clients. He sustained a head injury and is back home, totally dependent on his parents. The other one was the 22 year son of the manager at the Nashville studio we used to film the Federal video. His son was away at college in Texas and became paralyzed from the shoulders down just like Christopher Reeve after an automobile accident. He is wheelchair-bound and is back home with his parents. Then I say:

"The premiums for long-term care insurance are so inexpensive for young adults and at a time like that, you would want all the help you could get, right?"

The most important part . . .

HIT THE ONE-TIME OPPORTUNITY FOR SIMPLIFIED UNDERWRITING (OR GUARANTEED ACCEPTANCE, IF APPLICABLE) REALLY HARD.

Even employer audiences sometimes think it will come back around as they are so used to other benefits being available once a year in some type of open enrollment.

I always emphasize that we will explain this part to their employees as a gift from their employer, and it IS. There are so many younger people who could never get long-term care insurance in the open market due to excess weight or serious conditions like diabetes, strokes, or out of control hypertension or cholesterol.

Of course, you have to explain that family members have to go through full underwriting but they all have access to the group premium discount. (Some of the multi-life plans provide simplified underwriting for working spouses, so you can make a VERY big deal out of that if it applies to your case. **Remember, it is essential to get the spouse covered if at all possible in order to keep the employee at work in the event the spouse has a long-term care event.**)

Make sure everyone understands:

a) **that eligible dependents can apply even if the employee doesn't.** That gives me a great place to say that it's ok to have more than one long-term care insurance policy and that it's fine to "stack" this one on top of an earlier policy purchased. If you are offering personal consultations, it's also a good way to encourage the employee to reserve a personal consultation slot, so you can review the existing policy.

b) **that each applicant must complete an application.** There is no family application as is the case with some other types of insurance.

FEATURES AND BENEFITS

- This is a great place to explain the three types of payout (reimbursement, indemnity and cash). Of course, you can explain this part and weight the definition toward the type of plan you are offering as they all have their pros and cons...you know what they are:

⇒ **reimbursement:** rate stability as the plan won't pay more than the actual charge and policyholders have to file claims to claim the benefits

⇒ **indemnity:** the entire benefit is paid but claims for qualified caregivers still need to be filed

⇒ **cash:** no claims have to be filed and the insured can use the money however it is needed, including to pay informal caregivers. This can be especially helpful in rural areas when licensed caregivers can be difficult to find. (You should also explain that policyholders who hire informal caregivers will likely be responsible for the employer's contribution of the caregiver's Social Security, Medicare and state employment taxes. Remember Nannygate? I think we will be hearing stories of Eldergate in a few years…but with private enterprise, I'm sure a number of support services will spring up to handle this bookkeeping need.)

You can show the benefit options available for home care, facility care, lifetime maximum, inflation and waiting period but I strongly recommend that you let the employer know you will be showing four sample plans. That gives the employees a place to start so the decisions aren't overwhelming. We learned this in the Federal program and I've carried the idea through many enrollments.

The April 25, 2010 *CBS News Sunday Morning* with Charles Osgood did a segment on decision making and said that too many choices definitely decrease buying behavior. A company that makes jam tested this by putting 24 flavors on a display table and only six on another table. The table with the 24 flavors was mobbed by shoppers, but the results showed that shoppers were ten times more likely to buy from the table with the six flavors.

In our industry, even six would be too many. I offer four sample plans with the rates for ages 18-75 with inflation on one side of the page and without inflation (or the Guaranteed Purchase Option inflation benefit) on the other side. You can see samples in Appendix C.

Here are several configurations I've used, and on the page with inflation, you will notice the word "initial" before the benefit maximum. That word sets the stage to explain the inflation benefit.

CASH PLAN

Bronze: $3,000 home care/$4,000 facility, $100,000 initial benefit account = payout period of 33 months home care/25 months facility

Silver: $4500 home care/$6000 facility, $200,000 initial benefit account = payout period of 44 months home care/33 months facility

Gold: same except $300,000 initial benefit account = payout period of 66 months home care/50 months facility

Diamond: same except initial $500,000 benefit account = payout period of 9 years home care/7 years facility

Inflation option: 5% compound 2X

Rate tiers: Single, married or part of a couple

REIMBURSEMENT PLAN – MULTI-LIFE

Bronze: $100 daily benefit for all types of care, two year benefit period = initial benefit maximum $73,000

Silver: $120 daily benefit for all types of care, two year benefit period = initial benefit maximum $87,600

Gold: $130 daily benefit for all types of care, three year benefit period = initial benefit maximum $142,350

Diamond: $150 daily benefit for all types of care, four year benefit period = initial benefit maximum $219,000

Inflation option: 5% compound no max (the TN department of insurance would not approve a Partnership plan for this carrier with the 5% compound 2X option)

Rate tiers: Single, Married/Partner One Issued, Married/Partner Two Issued

REIMBURSEMENT PLAN – TRUE GROUP

Bronze: $100 daily benefit for all types of care, two year benefit period = initial benefit maximum $73,000

Silver: $150 daily benefit for all types of care, two year benefit period = initial benefit maximum $109,500

Gold: same except four year benefit period = initial benefit maximum $219,000

Diamond: $200 daily benefit for all types of care, four year benefit period = initial benefit maximum $292,000

Inflation option: 5% compound no max

Rate tier: no couples discount; same rates for all

When selecting your four plans, here are some things to think about:

- A 90 day waiting period is the most popular for worksite LTCI as most people worry more about needing help for three years, not three months.
- Inflation coverage is so important but with longer life spans, insurance carriers have raised the premium for the 5% annual compound inflation with no max benefit. Here are alternate ideas if the 5% compound no max is out of reach for most employees:
  ⇒ Consider that at 5% compounded annually, the benefit will double in 15 years. If you start someone at $3000 a month, how long will it take to become $12,000 a month? That's right…30 years. What if you started them at $6000 and offered a 5% compound 2x inflation option that will result in $12,000 in 15 years? Generally that plan is less expensive than $3000 a month and a 5% compound inflation no max. (If you are offering a Partnership plan, you will want to ask

the insurance carrier if your state allows the 5% compound 2x inflation option for applicants under age 61.)

⇒ You may be thinking, why wouldn't we just offer 3% compound no max? Remember how to determine how long it will take a benefit to double? That's right – divide it into 72 like this:

72 ÷ 5% = 14.5 years
72 ÷ 4% = 18 years
72 ÷ 3% = 24 years

⇒ So if you do 3% compound no max, you may be able to start the monthly benefit at $7500 for less premium than $4800 5% compound no max, and it will take 26 years before the $4800 catches up.

Anniversary	5% Compound No Max	3% Compound No Max
0	$4,800	$7,500
1	$5,040	$7,725
2	$5,292	$7,957
3	$5,557	$8,195
4	$5,834	$8,441
5	$6,126	$8,695
6	$6,432	$8,955
7	$6,754	$9,224
8	$7,092	$9,501
9	$7,446	$9,786
10	$7,819	$10,079
11	$8,210	$10,382
12	$8,620	$10,693
13	$9,051	$11,014
14	$9,504	$11,344
15	$9,979	$11,685
16	$10,478	$12,035
17	$11,002	$12,396
18	$11,552	$12,768
19	$12,129	$13,151
20	$12,736	$13,546
21	$13,373	$13,952
22	$14,041	$14,371
23	$14,743	$14,802
24	$15,480	$15,246
25	$16,255	$15,703

- Whichever inflation option you use, put a note at the bottom of the page about what will happen to the daily or monthly benefit and the benefit maximum – will it grow at 5% compound until it doubles then stop growing? Will it grow forever and double every 15 years as long as benefits have not been exhausted? On the page without inflation, put a clear note at the bottom that the benefits won't grow, or explain the Future Purchase Option.
- If you are offering a Partnership plan, put a note at the bottom of the non-inflation page that spells out the ramifications of not buying an inflation benefit at the appropriate age groups for your state.

SAMPLE PREMIUMS

In the employer presentation, I'll show one slide without inflation (or with the GPO method) for the four sample plans at age 30, 40, 50 and 60 and the next slide will show the premium with my primary inflation benefit. All of these premiums include the couple's discount if the carrier I'm using provides one. This provides a flavor of sample premiums.

Then I introduce my two favorite slides – the Quick Payback slide and the LTCI vs. Investing slide.

The Quick Payback slide multiplies the premium for the age 50 Silver plan x 30 years and compares the result with the daily or monthly benefit and total lifetime max at 30 years. Right below that, it divides the premium paid in 30 years by the daily or monthly benefit in 30 years and shows that all of the premium is paid back in a few months, if care is needed at that time. For example, if the monthly premium was $91.44 for a plan that will pay about two-thirds of the cost in the Southeast ($130 daily benefit/$4000 monthly benefit) with a three year benefit period and 5% compound no max inflation, the Quick Payback slide would look like this:

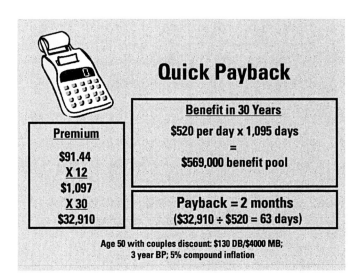

The policyholder spent about $33,000 to get a benefit pool of over half a million, and at claim time, the entire premium is paid back in only two months.

My second favorite slide is the LTCi vs. Investing. Investing the age 50 premium at an average annual return of 6% for a 30 year period earns $92,000 BEFORE taxes and investment fees vs. a GUARANTEED benefit pool of $569,000.

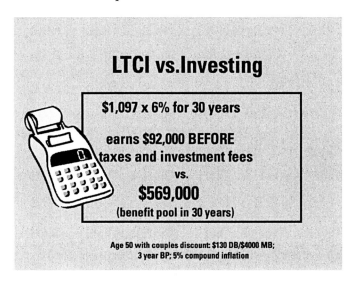

After making the Quick Payback and LTCi vs. Investing points, I can mention additional features that we can offer to the employees but I'm careful not to make them front and center as they can cause confusion. Here are my thoughts on what is generally available in the marketplace:

Shared waiver (waives the premium for both when only one goes on claim): If this benefit is only 1%-2% additional premium, I always include it. It's a meaningful benefit, sounds good, inexpensive, so why make the employees have to think about it?

Restoration of benefits (restores the benefits if the insured is no longer benefit eligible for at least 180 days): I rarely sold this benefit in the individual market as most older people never get better. In worksite, it is meaningful as young people can certainly recover after an accident, for example. It's especially meaningful for worksite age purchasers who can only afford a plan with a short benefit period. It doesn't cost much yet (like 2% - 8% depending on the benefit period). A couple of companies automatically include it, and it definitely has sizzle to be able to say that in the employee education meeting.

Survivor: This benefit generally costs about 9% and typically provides a paid-up policy for a surviving spouse/partner if the couple held the coverage at least ten years. Understand that if a couple buys the shared waiver benefit and the benefit-eligible partner dies, the premium will come back for the well spouse unless they have the survivor benefit. It isn't purchased a lot, but it's important to explain it in the personal consultation.

Shared care: I know many of us have been in love with this benefit in the individual market, but it doesn't get nearly as much play in worksite LTCI except perhaps with the executives. It's one more decision that has to be explained and unless you have a couple sitting in front of you in the personal consultation, it's difficult to include it routinely in the sale. One major company requires full underwriting for this benefit so that automatically shuts it down.

Accelerated payment (10 pay or pay to age 65): These plans are a very small portion of the market in general and microscopic in worksite due to affordability. It's nice to have them available though and occasionally, a serious planner will want it. A simple way to explain it is that the insured will generally pay the same premium in ten years that would be paid over a 30 year period based on issue age premium, but the main reason to do it is because it protects from class rate increases once the accelerated payment period has ended. It is also nice for the insured not to have to pay premium after retirement when most people are trying to decrease expenses.

Return of premium (with or without claims): This is another benefit that can be fun to talk about, but just like in the individual market, very few employees snap it up. In a personal consultation, it is simple to say that it's available but go into the "did you worry" close in Chapter Eleven, *What's In Your "Close" Closet?"* Having said that, I have noticed an uptick in the purchase of this benefit by employees who buy online without attending an employee education meeting or having a personal consultation.

Nonforfeiture: I've never been a fan of this benefit and even though it has decreased dramatically in price with many carriers, I'm still not big on it and advise employees to spend their precious insurance dollars elsewhere. This is especially true since most carriers include contingent nonforfeiture as we discussed earlier. That means the insured will get it anyway if premium goes up a pre-defined amount in a lifetime. The Office of Personnel Management made a conscious decision not to offer it in the Federal program, and I was so relieved as it is so complicated to explain. It is required to offer it in a multi-life sale since it is still an individual product, but an employer can decide not to offer it with a true group product. Consequently, I don't like it when a true group carrier tells me it is hard-wired into the website and must be offered even if I could get the employer to decide not to offer it. It just provides one more way uneducated employees can make mistakes in spending their premium dollars wisely, especially when enrolling online.

HOW TO ENROLL

Worksite LTCI is a mixture of paper and online enrollment at this point. True group is online and a couple of the multi-life carriers do online enrollment. I was one of the biggest advocates for this until I actually did some cases with it. The downfall happens when employees who haven't attended meetings or personal consultations enroll online and do things like buy return of premium, accelerated premium and / or nonforfeiture and don't buy an inflation benefit. I can't begin to tell you the hours we've spent personally contacting these employees and showing them how to reallocate their premium dollars and buy something that is much better for them. And of course, they don't all listen to our advice, so I know some of them will be really disappointed at claim time. In a true group situation, the carrier may not disclose by name which employees bought which benefit, so the producer can't reach out to them to get them to change their mind.

I will talk about the large true group enrollments in Chapter Nine, *You Hooked Moby Dick-Now What?* but in this chapter, let me speak to the smaller multi-life enrollments which can still require paper applications for enrollment.

Simplified underwriting is helpful in the enrollment process, since there are only a handful of questions to answer, but family members and sometimes the spouse or partner is required to go through full underwriting. To facilitate this process, I've gone so far as to hand out instructions on how to complete the application and have included samples of this work for you in Appendix D. You will see that these instructions even go through the personal worksheet since that is a requirement with most enrollments now.

Here's the process in a nutshell with paper applications or a combination of paper and online:

1) Make sure the last slide in your employee presentation has a strong call to action to enroll during the time frame that allows the underwriting concession and to sign up for a personal consultation if you are offering them.
2) Offer applications for pickup at the end of the employee meeting.
3) Have the employer post the applications and the enrollment instructions on the benefits website.
4) Leave plenty of applications with the HR contact for employees to pick up.
5) If applicable, make sure the rate pages for the four sample plans contains the URL for the personal consultations and for the online enrollment.

Both employers and employees alike are very interested to hear when this coverage is totally portable. It always is with multi-life since that is an individual product and it is with most true group products. For the record, I wouldn't sell a group program that isn't totally portable. It's so important for these policies to follow the employee at the same premium and same benefits.

When you explain the portability, that's also a great place to mention that the premium can only increase on a class basis. I usually follow this statement that if a class rate increase is worrisome, some people take advantage of the accelerated payment option (if there is one), as the employees who are most likely to take advantage of that are probably sitting in front of you.

EMPLOYEE COMMUNICATION PROCESS - THE MOST IMPORTANT PART

You can't complete any employer presentation without covering the employee education process and securing the total commitment to conduct this process appropriately. Let me say this as plainly as I can.

If you don't get anything else out of this book, this is the section to which you should pay the most attention.

Explain how important it is to conduct a thorough six to eight week employee education process that requires:

- an announcement letter to the homes;
- a seven educational email campaign that provides the employee education about long-term care insurance in "sound-bytes";
- one hour employee meetings on-the-clock (45 minutes for the presentation and 15 for Q&A) and you can offer to do a Family Night meeting with pizza if the employer thinks this will appeal to employees;
- the employer to post all of the educational materials on the company website (important: find out if this website is accessible outside of the workplace; i.e. can the spouse and other family members get to it?)
- permission to hold personal consultations on-the-clock;
- payroll deduction;
- permission to use the company logo on the educational materials; and
- private conference rooms for the personal consultations.

My philosophy on the employee education process is for the employee not to hear anything new at the employee education meeting as they've already heard the information in pieces during the education process. The meeting just solidifies and reinforces the information.

You should also ask how the employer communicates with the employees and utilize any other channels that are available which can include:

- an article in the employee magazine
- webinars (especially for other locations)
- if the company website isn't accessible outside of the workplace, you can offer to provide CDs of the employee education presentation that the employees can request from the HR department.

Make it clear to the employer that your goal is to make sure the employees understand what a gift from the employer the long-term care insurance offering represents; in other words, you will make the employer look like a hero!

We will discuss this education process in detail in the next chapter but now let me share some very hard lessons I've learned along the way.

1) **Spell out the education process in writing and get the employer to agree to it with a signature of the top decision maker before you agree to do the enrollment.** This list of employee education steps should be spelled out with exact dates as to when each step will occur.

2) **Make absolutely sure the seven educational emails will be sent out.** Don't agree to just have them posted on a site that the employees go to for education.

Identify who will be sending them out at that stage and get that person or department's commitment. One of our early enrollments was ruined because the IT department decided after the 3rd email to send only one more and combined #4 - #7. These comprise the meat of the education and since this combination email largely went unread, the enrollment results were much lower than they would have been.

3) **Don't give copies of the seven emails to anyone in the initial employer presentation before the case is sold.** It's too easy for them to wind up in the hands of a competitor who promises to emulate the employee education process you explained. In the employer presentation, all you are doing is referencing the topic of each email so the decision makers can see the purpose of sending them out:

- *What is Long-Term Care?* (dismantles the myth that long-term care is nursing home insurance for old people)
- *What Are the Odds I Will Need LTC?* (explains how common it is to need at least home care and compares the risk to other common risks that are much lower than this one but we would never think of not insuring)
- *Who Pays for Long-Term Care?* (eliminates the misconceptions about health insurance or Medicare covering long-term care and touches on the limitations and spend-down requirements of Medicaid; also introduces the Partnership if you are offering one)
- *How Does a Long-Term Care Need Affect My Lifestyle?* (hits hard on the traumatic and often devastating impact long-term care has on lifestyle and the entire family)
- *How Does Long-Term Care Insurance Work?* (introduces the local cost of care and defines long-term care insurance terms such as daily or monthly benefit, benefit maximum, inflation benefit, elimination (waiting) period, types of care covered)
- *What Are My Benefit Choices For My Personal LTC Insurance Plan?* (introduces the four sample plans; illustrates sample premium for a 35 and 45 year old and compares paying premium for 30 years vs. benefit in 30 years; illustrates true cost of waiting from 35 to 45)

- *Should I Obtain Long-Term Care Insurance For My Parents or Adult Children?* (The first sentence says "Only if you value your lifestyle." Enough said.)

TIMING OF THE ENROLLMENT

What about timing of the enrollment? Off-cycle is best, hands down. There is such an educational curve to a long-term care insurance offering and other benefits can be distracting. That said, one of our most successful enrollments was on-cycle and the reasons I agreed to it were:

1) The HR director already owned LTCI and was one of the biggest proponents I had ever met for long-term care insurance.

2) She allowed the full pre-education campaign including a 45 minute employee meeting on the benefits day, and as many personal consultations as the employees asked for.

3) the employer was introducing health savings accounts and contributing $150 a month into the HSA for each employee. And – get this – this HR director also allowed the employees to take advantage of the 8% savings available by electing the annual premium mode. She did this by allowing the HSA employer contribution to be advanced and fund the annual premium. That provided a way for employees to buy LTCI with pre-tax dollars while receiving the savings from paying annually, so it was a home run.

In closing the employer education, I like to emphasize that long-term care is the *real* health care crisis in America and that the best way to solve it is to provide coverage with pennies on the dollar through insurance instead of paying the full price with higher taxes. In a nutshell, long-term care insurance supports:

- family caregiving
- labor force participation
- solvency of public programs
- avoidance of excessive taxation

What's not to love about a program that does all these things?

IMPLEMENTATION ISSUES

PAYROLL CALL

This is SUCH an important component of a smooth implementation. Don't ever let either an insurance carrier or employer or anyone else talk you out of having it. Not doing it can come back to haunt you so quickly!

This is a call between the insurance carrier's payroll department and the employer's payroll department. Make sure the contacts by name are clearly identified on each side. Then have the carrier payroll contact walk through the process with the employer payroll contact so all is understood up front.

Why is this call so important? It is the employer's first contact with the insurance company, so there is a strong public relations element involved here. The relationship can go south in a hurry if the payroll contact from the carrier is very task-oriented and makes the employer feel that they have to rigidly comply with the carrier's way of doing things. (Can you tell I've learned this the hard way?) Work with your marketing contacts to be sure this doesn't happen, and if it ever does, make sure the carrier knows about it and that you will never accept that person on a payroll call again.

Each carrier has a payroll form for the employer to complete to indicate preferences such as how to receive the monthly billing statement – electronically, paper, fax – and how the employer will submit the premium – wire transfer, check, etc. But completing the form isn't enough. The phone call is crucial to eliminate employer misunderstandings about the long-term care insurance enrollment process, which is quite different than any other employee benefit.

EFFECTIVE DATES

For example, just nailing down the effective date of coverage can be a big deal. It's not unusual for either an employer or benefits consultant to ask for an effective date two weeks after the proposal is due. Long-term care insurance doesn't work this way. Some carriers won't make the coverage effective until one payroll deduction cycle has been completed and the money sent to the insurance company. This is called "pre-paid insurance". Another carrier might make the coverage effective as soon as the application is approved and wait for the money to come in from the first payroll deduction cycle.

Since so much of long-term care insurance requires some level of underwriting, it's an educational curve for employers to understand it isn't usually one blanket effective date for everyone. Only employees who answer "no" to all of the simplified underwriting questions can be effective on the same date; all other applicants will be effective as the underwriting process is completed. This nearly always involves a telephone call and can involve ordering medical records and even a personal visit. You can request a first of the month effective date for the employees who are accepted immediately but that's about the best you can do.

This is also the time to establish how new hires will be handled as that is one of the questions on the payroll form. Some carriers allow an annual open enrollment for new hires vs. providing a defined period of time after the date of hire for the new employee to take advantage of the underwriting concession. I prefer this annual event as it provides a much better opportunity to do the necessary pre-education and get in front on the new hires to be sure they understand the gift of being able to enroll in this very special benefit without having to go through full underwriting. You just have to be sure you set the reminder in your contact manager to get the list of new hires in plenty of time to start the pre-education before the annual date.

The employer should agree to have the payroll deduction apply to the employee and the spouse. Other family members will be handled outside of this process, but this doesn't prevent employees from paying their premium if they desire to do so. There is an alternate billing block on the application and the bills can be sent to anyone.

It's also a good time during the call to ask the employer if the premium can be equally deducted over at least two paychecks during the month instead of coming out of one paycheck, unless employees are paid monthly, of course. This will drive up participation as it makes it much easier for employees to buy long-term care insurance.

EMPLOYER CONTRIBUTION

It's always wonderful to have an employer contribution, especially if it applies to every employee. If that's the case, the insurance carrier will provide the monthly list bill to the employer and the employer will payroll deduct only the premium that exceeds the employer contribution.

However, one of the tax incentives for LTCI is that an employer can choose to pay the premium for some, not all employees, if the employees are segmented by class, such as job title, salary, or tenure. If this is the case, the insurance carrier can provide one bill for the list of employees the employer is paying for and a separate bill for the voluntary enrollment. If there is a savings to pay annually, you might see the employer want to pay the executives' premium once a year, and do the list bill, payroll deduction process only on the voluntary offering.

I think you can see by now the number of important decisions that are covered on the payroll call and why this call is such an essential component of a successful implementation. One parting tip is to either **be on the call yourself or have a trusted person on your staff on the call.** That way you can make sure the customer service level is maintained and if anything starts to go wrong, you have a chance to step in and either prevent it or contain the damage.

CHAPTER SIX

BUILDING BLOCKS OF THE ESSENTIAL EMPLOYEE EDUCATION STRATEGY

Once you have the green light and full support from management to do the employee education the way you know it needs to be done, you can breathe a huge sigh of relief. Then you can devote your energy to this crucial process. To make this meaningful to you, I want you to think of this process as throwing out life preservers to drowning people, because that's exactly what you are doing!

Without long-term care insurance, families are going to suffer incredibly when a loved one needs long-term care. You have the power to prevent much of this suffering by how well you conduct the employee education effort.

Resist the urge to do what much of the industry has done.

Don't emphasize financial protection as the #1 point.

The most important point in this entire process is:

Buying long-term care insurance is how we take care of our families in this century!!

81

I learned this at the first employee education meeting that we did at Pearl Harbor as part of the Federal program employee education effort.

It was about two minutes before the meeting was to start. I noticed a young soldier in the audience sitting alone. I went to him, introduced myself and made sure he understood this was a long-term care insurance meeting. He assured me he knew what it was. I quickly responded with "I am SO glad you are here, but do you mind telling me why you are here? What was your motivation to come?" His answer changed the entire focus of our educational outreach, not just for the Federal program but for every enrollment we've done since and all the speeches I've given on this topic from that moment forward. He in essence said, "I'm here because here in Hawaii, we really believe in taking care of our families. We don't move away. It's so hard to keep this promise today with the cost of living and so many conflicting demands. We see this insurance as the way to keep that promise." I communicated his answer to the rest of our 16 person team and this became the #1 message. The financial took a back seat. It became an "oh by the way" statement. We said "Long-term care insurance is how we take care of our families today and oh by the way, you also get to protect your savings."

Because of all the compliance issues and attorneys scrubbing the consumer information, the compassion and emotion has been largely driven out of the long-term care insurance presentation. I urge you to put it back in, especially in worksite. If you emphasize just the financial side, I can assure you many employees can't identify with that. They are trying to get from day to day to meet the current financial obligations of taking care of a family and educating their children.

What they can identify with is how this insurance allows them to take care of their families. When I started selling long-term care insurance in 1988, the most common objection I heard was "My kids will take care of me." The baby boomer prospects we are talking with now are those kids and the first thing on their minds is they don't ever want their kids to go through what they just went through or are going through. And guess what, it's not just the baby boomers who are thinking that way.

We had finished the onsite personal consultation meetings at a large employer, and I took a call from an employee who hadn't been able to make those but wanted a phone consultation. In my preliminary fact finding, I learned that he was 27 years old and his wife was 24. A little surprised at his level of interest in this benefit, I went on to ask my customary question of why he was interested. His answer was another one that put a laser eye on what we are doing here. He said "My father just had a stroke and moved in with us. I have a four-year-old son. I don't want him to EVER go through this."

If you wind up using my employee education presentation, you will reach out to families with compassion and caring and offer them a lifeline to keeping their lifestyle and goals in place if they become a caregiver as this young couple has. To do this, I encourage you to not be afraid to share a personal long-term care story if you have one or someone else's if you don't. Too often (myself included) it can be difficult to talk about emotional issues in front of an audience or with people you don't know very well.

Get over it.

The stakes are too high with this topic to back off from these stories. I want you to understand that …

Every long-term care insurance policy you sell has the power to change the life of that family for generations to come.

Remember the first Michael J. Fox "Back to the Future" movie? It flashed back to what life could have been like if the dad ("George Fly") hadn't stood up to the bully ("Biff") and married the girl who became the mother of Michael J. Fox's character. Without long-term care insurance, many, many families will lose dignity and relationships will suffer. Marriages will break up. Siblings won't talk to each other ever again because the burden fell unfairly on one. Parent and adult child relationships will be changed forever as the adult child changes from the son or daughter to the primary caregiver who has to personal things like help with bathing, dressing and toileting for a parent who would have never wanted that. Children will be deprived of the opportunity to attend the college of their choice because the money had to go to keep dad at home after his accident or mom at home after her stroke. Or they won't go to college because they need to stay home and take care of the parent in the long-term care situation so the other parent can continue to work.

Did you read the *Washington Post* article that said over one million children under age 18 function as caregivers? Here's an excerpt:

> *As many as 1.4 million children in the United States from age 8 to 18 care for a chronically ill or disabled relative, according to a 2005 survey by the United Hospital Fund and the National Alliance for caregiving. Children provide companionship, run errands and balance checkbooks. Some change feeding tubes or adult diapers.*[34]

The 18 year old girl in the story is a freshman in college and immediately goes home after her classes to take care of her mother who has MS. She bathes her, prepares her meals, empties her catheter bag and gives her two dozen kinds of medication. She helps take care of a 9 year old cousin as well by getting him off to school.

Hopefully by now you are seeing the mission in conducting a phenomenal employee education effort with each enrollment, and we can get back to the practical steps.

THE EMPLOYEE EDUCATION TIME TABLE

Once the earliest effective date desired by the employer has been agreed to, that drives the time table for the employee education program. You back up eight weeks prior to that date and it usually goes like this:

Long-Term Care Insurance Employee Education Outreach	
	Meeting with Management to Obtain Approval
Employee Communications	Post the Announcement Letter and Articles 1-7 on company website.
Week 1	Announcement Letter to Homes
Week 2	Email/Article 1 *What is Long-Term Care?* **Put up posters with meeting schedule**
Week 3	Email/Article 2 *Who Pays for Long-Term Care?*
Week 4	Email/Article 3 *What Are the Odds I Will Need Long-Term Care?*
Week 5	Email/Article 4 *How Will a Long-Term Care Need Affect My Lifestyle?*
Week 6	Email/Article 5 *How Does Long-Term Care Insurance Work?*
Week 7	Email/Article 6 *What Are My Benefit Choices for My Personal LTC Insurance Plan?*
Week 8	Email/Article 7 *Should I Obtain Long-Term Care Insurance for My Parents or Adult Children?*

Open Enrollment	
Week 9	**Open Enrollment Begins** **Seminars for Employees, Retirees & Their Families**
Week 10	**Personal Consultations**
Week 11	**Reminder Notice to Employees**
Week 12	**30-day Open Enrollment Concluded (applications accepted thereafter with full medical questions)**
On-Going Services	
	Toll-free Customer Support **Web Resources** **On-going Enrollment** **New Employee Enrollment**

This is the standard schedule that I show an employer, then we customize it to that employer's environment. For example, if it is higher education (or any type of school system), you wouldn't want to have the employee meetings conflicting with finals week or graduation. Some teaching colleges have the faculty work year round but if most of the faculty doesn't work during the summer, you have to make the open enrollment period happen before the mad rush of activity to complete a semester or school year.

A compressed enrollment schedule can be accomplished in this way but not any shorter:

Week 1: Announcement letter mailed to homes on Monday and Email #1 goes out on Thursday.
Week 2: Email #2 on Tuesday and Email #3 on Friday
Week 3: Email #4 on Wednesday
Week 4: Email #5 on Tuesday
Week 5: Email #6 on Tuesday
Week 6: Email #7 on Monday and the employee meetings can start

on Wednesday, and this week is the first week of the 30 day open enrollment period for underwriting concessions.

Each communication piece (the announcement letter, posters, the seven educational emails) should all include these essential pieces of information:

- the one-time opportunity for the open enrollment with the exact dates and whether that means limited questions or guaranteed acceptance;
- the employee education meeting schedule (date, time, location); and
- family members are welcome at meetings and personal consultations.

If this is a large group and there are many employee meetings, you can include the URL to the website that shows the entire schedule instead of including it in your communication pieces.

With email #4, I also reference the ability to sign up for a personal consultation. If you are providing a website to sign up for these, you should provide that URL on each remaining email.

If you are doing a true group enrollment and the carrier is mailing information to the homes, ask the carrier to include the meeting schedule on each piece, in addition to the URL for the personal consultation signup page if you are using one.

A broker brought me a prestigious medical teaching college that wanted long-term care insurance. The HR staff was clear in letting me know that the doctors rarely attended employee meetings. To overcome this, I decided to call the personal consultations "private consultations" and added a sentence at the end of each educational email: "Can't come to a meeting? Sign up for a private consultation at [URL]."

My thinking was that it would make the doctors feel special and that they were getting preferential treatment. The broker helped by speaking for a few minutes at the physician faculty meeting and mentioning that private consultations were available. Guess what – it worked! Just as the HR staff had predicted, most didn't come to the meetings, but many of them did sign up for a private consultation. This enrollment was very successful (example #3 in Chapter One) but my favorite memory was the last day of open enrollment. The waiting room was full of doctors in white coats waiting their turn. Imagine this for a minute. Doctors waiting on US. It was a clinic in reverse. Invariably, some were late which threw off the schedule for everyone else. We were stepping into the waiting room and sweetly saying "Oh doctor, I'm so sorry you had to wait. Please come back – I can see you now." Most of them were smiling as they could see the humor in the situation as we were really saying "See how it feels?" A few missed the humor altogether...but it wasn't lost on most of us, including the HR staff!

POSTERS:

I really like to have posters scattered around if there are places to post them at the worksite. I use emotional posters with messages like these:

The impact of taking care of family members.

"Is Your Lifestyle Important to You? Then you need to be sure your parents and in-laws have long-term care insurance. Pay the premium if you have to. It's much less expensive than providing the care yourself (especially if it means you have to give up your job or go part-time), or paying someone else to provide it at $5,000 a month or more."

LTC can happen at any age.

"Don't Gamble With Your Family's Financial Security. Did you know that long-term care at home is not covered by your group health insurance and that 40% of those needing long-term care often because of a traumatic accident or chronic illness are under age 65?"

Most long-term care happens at home and it's expensive.

"Keep What You've Worked For. At $3,000 - $6000 a month, how long could you pay for extended care at home? Protect yourself and the people you love from the tremendous sacrifice long-term care means to a family."

All of my posters end with "Long-Term Care Insurance: It's *lifestyle insurance* for you and your family."

I think you get the picture. No mention of nursing homes, and there is a major emphasis on the fact that anyone can need long-term care, at any age, and when it happens, it's really hard on a family.

The actual employee education presentation follows the same format as the employer presentation, except it is customized for the actual product that you wind up using, and it doesn't contain the section on the employee education process. So it is a three-part presentation. You can review the preceding chapter to review Part One and Part Two.

Part One: Clearing up the Myths
Part Two: The long-term care issue and why long-term care insurance is needed
Part Three: The plan offered by the employer
  › who is eligible
  › underwriting concession and open enrollment period dates
  › how to get a claim paid

90

> three benefit decisions (daily or monthly benefit, lifetime max, inflation)
> payout method and only the version that applies to their product is shown (reimbursement, indemnity or cash)
> the importance of the home care benefit (nursing home avoidance and can prevent family members from doing personal things for you)
> the importance of assisted living facility coverage (spouses can stay together/single people no longer have to worry about upkeep of a home)
> explanation that a major claim study has shown that the full duration of qualified care is paid for 85% of policyholders with a four year benefit
> the four sample plans (benefits and rates with couples discount forage 30, 40, 50 and 60)
> waiting period (explaining if it days to wait or if charges must be incurred)
> additional options (lightly mention and encourage them to sign up for a personal consultation to have a plan customized to their budget)
> Quick payback and LTCI vs Investing examples (I show a 40 year old paying premium for 40 years for this presentation.)
> payment methods (payroll deduction for employee and spouse; direct bill others)
> portability and rate increases only on a class basis
> wind up by emphasizing importance of getting coverage for anyone they think they might wind up taking care of, including adult children, if thesepeople are insurable now
> leave them with this contrast:
>> Long-term care insurance can mean a comfortable and secure life and retirement
>> Not having long-term care insurance can mean

a life caring for someone else's need, day in and day out.

› call to action: sign up for a personal consultation (family members are welcome) and/or pick up an application and/or enroll online. You can use a paper form that allows them to sign up for a personal consultation, especially for small groups. Make sure you put the form in the back of the room as they leave, not in the front of the room where you are. Ideally someone will be standing by the form to ensure that employees see it as they leave. Alternatively, some producers use an employee response form which allows the employees to say they want to be contacted to schedule a consultation, and that's fine. It's just more work and rather than chase them down, I like for employees to sign up on the spot for the consultation.

To reinforce the messages in the presentation, here is a list of handouts that we use with every enrollment.

HANDOUTS

- **Lifestyle Insurance brochure** - a brochure that promotes long-term care insurance as Lifestyle Insurance. It contains two emotional scenarios so that what we are talking about becomes more real to the employees and they can imagine themselves in a similar situation:

  1) younger person scenario:

  Carol, age 34, has a husband and two small children and works full-time as a teller at a local bank. She is in a car accident, and is now in a coma. Her doctor says she could be in a coma indefinitely. Carol's husband, Don, is shocked to learn that the bank's medical insurance won't pay for someone to care for Carol while he is at work.

Will Don be able to pay someone to care for Carol at the average of almost $70,000 per year and support the family on his pay alone – day care for the children, college education savings, car loan, rent, mortgage, and everyday living expenses?

2) becoming a caregiver for an older person:

Both Bob and Mary work full-time. With two children in college and one in high school, that's understandable! They are keeping up just fine, until Mary's father, who has always been in good health, has an unexpected stroke. After a short hospital stay, he is admitted to a skilled nursing facility to help him recover from the stroke. Mary can't believe it when she learns that Medicare and his Medicare supplement stop paying after about five weeks of care in the skilled nursing facility, after which her father has stabilized. In fact, he is recovered enough to stay home as long as there is someone around. He waits anxiously for Mary to take him home.

- *Will Mary quit her full-time job to care for her father?*

- *Will she go part-time? Now the expenses that she and Bob must meet are greater because elder care needs are added to college tuition needs.*

See what I mean about reinforcing that this insurance is how we take care of our families today? So many baby boomers find themselves in Mary's position. How can they take care of a parent and their own immediate family at the same time?

Or a spouse like Carol? One of the most devoted long-term care insurance producers I know is Kathy Halverson. Her story is in my original book **Long-Term Care: Your Financial Planning Guide** and in our NAIC-DRA Partnership training course, but it is included here for those of you who haven't seen it.

Kathy Halverson's 41-year-old husband was diagnosed in 1986 with Parkinson's disease. An insurance professional in Wisconsin, he and Kathy "had it all" when it came to insurance policies...all except long-term care insurance. Kathy had to learn the insurance business and take over his practice to care for him and provide for their family, especially their children's education. Her husband has since passed away, and Kathy has dedicated herself to getting the word out about how long-term care insurance can protect families. She repeatedly testifies, "We sold insurance for 31 years! We had it all . . . but not LTC . . . and after spending all our pensions, retirement, etc, to care for my husband and educate our children, we were 10 months away from seeking assistance [with Medicaid]."

Unlike Kim's story in the Introduction, Kathy and her husband did NOT have long-term care insurance because at age 41, they thought they were too young. If you ever want to hear first-hand the sacrificial consequences of that decision, talk to Kathy Halverson. She will be glad to talk with you, as her mission in life has become to prevent others from experiencing the trauma of a spouse having a long-term care need without the help of long-term care insurance.

It's not always about the money...

Something we lose sight of all too often...it's not just about money. No amount of money will help if you can't find caregivers. Don't forget that most long-term care insurance carriers have incredible care coordinators on staff, usually Registered Nurses, who work with the family to get their loved one initially certified for benefits, then to help find caregivers to carry out the plan of care. This is a free service as these nurses are employed by the insurance company, but there may even be a benefit to hire a private care coordinator, someone who doesn't work for the insurance company.

- One-page Medicaid eligibility guidelines: You might think this is a strange handout but I developed it when I first started selling long-term care insurance because I found that Medicaid was my real competition, not other insurance carriers. I found that if I take the mystery out of Medicaid, people no longer see it as a viable payer for long-term care. Today I have the estate recovery requirements printed from the Tennessee Medicaid website on the back side of this page. I also include an article that ran in the Nashville newspaper about how estate recovery is affecting family homes and farms.

If the enrollment is using a Partnership product, I also attach the consumer education handout from the Tennessee Department of Insurance website about the Tennessee Partnership. You can print out similar materials from your state insurance department. If you take our Partnership training course at www.LTCiTraining.com, all of the specific state Partnership documents are included, in addition to the one-page Medicaid eligibility sheet for all of the states in which you elect to be certified.

- The insurance company product brochure (provided by the insurance company)

- The NAIC Long-Term Care Insurance Shopper's Guide (provided by the insurance company)

- The rate sheet for the four sample plans (I suggest holding this back until the end so the attendees don't study it and not pay attention to the presentation.)

- Optional: Some employers want a record of who was at the meeting as well as wanting something in the personnel file that long-term care insurance was offered in the event an employee has a long-term care event and tries to say the benefit wasn't offered. Some producers love to use this form as it forces a decision about the interest level. You can lay it out so they let you know they are signing up for a personal consultation or you can set the form up to allow you to call them and set up an appointment yourself if you prefer.

LONG-TERM CARE INSURANCE RESPONSE FORM

☐ YES – I'm interested in long-term care insurance.

☐ For myself

☐ For myself and my spouse

☐ For a family member or friend

I am signing up for a personal consultation.

Alternate: Call me to set up a personal consultation

Company ext. _____

Home telephone _____

Best time to call _____A.M. _____P.M.

Name _____

— —

☐ I'm not interested in long-term care insurance.

I, _____, affirm that I have been presented with information regarding long-term care insurance through my employer, name of company. I have been informed of the risk of needing and the annually increasing costs of home health care, assisted living, adult day care and nursing home are and the ability to protect my care choices and my net worth through the purchase of long-term care insurance. I have chosen not to purchase long-term care insurance and have agreed to self-insure the risk of long-term care.

Signature _____

Print Name _____

Date _____

(Name of Employer)

CLOSING OUT THE EMPLOYEE EDUCATION MEETING.

- Hand out the rate sheet and show the attendees how to find their age and their spouse's age in order to determine the monthly premium.
- Tell them the premium will be divided between their paychecks (if this is true).
- Tell them how to enroll: online, paper apps or a choice if they have one. If it is online and they have to print out the spouse or family member app, let them know that so they aren't expecting a 100% online enrollment experience.
- Mention the Family Night seminar if you are holding one.
- Encourage them to sign up for a personal consultation either with the paper signup sheet that you are providing or point them to the URL at the bottom of the rate sheet so they can go online and sign up for one.
- Encourage them to bring spouses/partners and any other interested family members to the personal consultations or another meeting. Offer to do a phone consultation if they prefer for those family members.
- If the product is available to their family members in other states, mention this if you haven't already. Some carriers with online enrollment even have a place on the website to email family members so they can see the education, benefit options, rate calculator, and apply for the coverage at the group discount.

Most of all, encourage the attendees to ask all the other employees they work with to come to a meeting and/or sign up for a personal consultation.

Answer questions as time permits or steer them to sign up for a personal consultation to get all their questions answered.

At this point, if someone doesn't ask the question "What if I never need it?" I will bring it up and go through the answer which is in Chapter Eleven, *What's In Your "Close" Closet?*

We Hit the Nail on the Head With This Solution

We were enrolling a large employer and found out that only the employees could see the employee website while they were at work. They had no access to it from home so while we had the educational materials on the employee website, we knew that wouldn't benefit the spouses and other family members.

So we recorded the employee presentation education and provided HR with a couple of hundred CDs. They went like hotcakes, especially as we had a slide at the end of the live presentation that let employees know they could pick them up in HR for their family members.

Today, anyone can do this as there is a "Record Narration" command under "Slide Show" in the Microsoft PowerPoint program for versions 2003 and on. You can record one slide at a time until you have the entire presentation recorded, then burn it to a CD. If you need hundreds like we did, take it to a CD duplicator. They're fast and very inexpensive compared to the return you will get on all the extra policies they will sell for you!

CHAPTER SEVEN

PRECIOUS MOMENTS: THE PERSONAL CONSULTATION

The name of this chapter comes from the love that I have for doing personal consultations. This is the chance to see the employees one-on-one and hear their stories. I love it, because it's my chance to impact their lives forever. My goal in this chapter is by the end of it, you too will see these times in the same light – as a precious opportunity to reach out and touch a family in a very caring, compassionate way in order to persuade them to make a purchase that will bring dignity and the utmost relief to their family at a time that could otherwise be one of the toughest experiences they will ever have to deal with as a family.

I balance this with the critics of our industry who paint caregiving as an awesome privilege and say that caregivers rarely complain. These critics try to make us feel guilty for bringing up an insurance sale, of all things. I have my Google search engine set to deliver all the articles about long-term care to my email box on a daily basis. It's a growing subject, and this is why I consistently stare at 200+ emails every day and have the feeling that I am digging in sand as I try to actually read all these articles in a timely fashion.

The discouraging articles are the countless caregiver articles that never mention long-term care insurance. I even read caregiving literature and reports published by some of the same insurance companies that offer long-term care insurance and never see it mentioned once. I know these are large insurance companies but really...how can they write a report on caregiving and not even mention the private sector's solution to paying for it?

A public entity like PBS can be somewhat excused because they don't know. I was thrilled to be a small part of a PBS documentary called "And Thou Shalt Honor" which aired in 2002. They had hours of footage of caregiving material with nothing about how care is financed. There was a plan, however, to include a few minutes from a long-term care insurance consumer seminar that was to be held in the Washington, DC area. At the last minute, the producer holding it was unable to get enough of an audience to pull it off.

I got an emergency call on a Thursday about this situation because the hotel had been booked, the film crew was lined up, and it was going to be expensive to change the plans. I was traveling insanely that year, but because they were willing to hold it two days later on Saturday, I was able to hop a plane and do it for them. The audience was staged with some of the film crew and a few local consumer advocates but what happened was really interesting.

The audience went from being a staged situation to being genuinely interested in the topic. Most of them shared personal long-term care stories in taped interviews after I finished the consumer seminar. The PBS producers were shaking their heads as they wondered aloud how so little of the information I had shared about the lack of financing available for LTC was public knowledge. To their credit, they built in much more information on long-term care insurance into the documentary once they truly understood it is the best option to pay for long-term care for those who want to make their own care decisions.

So I try to tell myself that all the articles about caregiving that either ignore long-term care insurance or say disparaging things about it are just written by people who have not been fortunate enough to hear from someone with firsthand information about long-term care insurance who has seen its phenomenal impact on a family. That's why I'm so excited to talk to producers in this book as I know so many of you will be the mouthpiece to provide this desperately needed information to the families in your community. For many years, that information could be provided in community seminars as I did in the early years of my long-term care insurance practice. Today, however, the easiest place to get the word out is in the workplace.

Everything I've said about the employee education process to this point is really important to make that happen, but it's the personal consultations that complete the process and provide the high participation rates that I shared with you in Chapter One. We've done enrollments with and without them, and the ones with them are far more successful. You can't do them with large groups, you say? Size-wise, we've done them from 10 – 5,500 employees which takes in most sizes that you will be dealing with. The 5,500 employee group had 98% of the employees all in one state, so we were able to do the consultations in five locations and handle the rest via telephone consultations.

With the new technology like "Go to Meeting", you can do a personal consultation for anyone or an employee education meeting for any group of employees. They can see your computer screen and you can show them anything you want them to see from the presentation to the rate software or the online enrollment site.

So with most of your sales, you will have the opportunity to do personal consultations.

THE ANATOMY OF THE PERSONAL CONSULTATION

The first thing I do is to warmly welcome the people into my conference room. After all, they made the effort to sign up for this spot so this is important to them. I have them sit next to me so they can see my computer screen, not across from me. I say "Tell me about yourself – why are you interested in long-term care insurance?"

And that is the most important question you will ask all day. Whatever the answer is tells you why they will enroll in the plan (or apply, if it has any level of underwriting).

Then I tell them I have to start off with some personal questions. Here is the list and why I ask them:

- Your birthdate and age (This lets me know if there is an imminent birthday.)
- What do you do for the company? (This helps me have an idea about affordability and helps establish rapport. I might ask how long they've worked there and do my best to make them feel great about the importance of their contribution to the company.)
- Are you married? If so, spouse birthdate and age (This sets the stage that the spouse will apply – no question.)
- (*If spouses have to go through underwriting*): Any health issues with your spouse? Does he or she take any medication? Approximate height and weight?
- Does your spouse work? Some carriers offer underwriting concessions for working spouses so I definitely need to know if that is the case; otherwise, I'm asking to get an idea for affordability purposes.)
- Do you have children? Names, how old are they and what are they doing? (I'm identifying adult children for whom they may wish to buy a policy if they would be responsible for this child's caregiving needs.)

- Grandchildren? (I may bring them into the discussion when we talk about their thoughts about their children or grandchildren being responsible for their care someday.)
- Do you plan on staying in this area? (That helps me know the daily or monthly benefit level to recommend.)
- Do you have longevity in your family? (This helps me with the lifetime maximum recommendation.)
- Do you have Alzheimer's in your family? (This helps with the lifetime maximum recommendation. I get the answer to this and the preceding question for the spouse/partner as well.)
- Were you able to make it to an employee education meeting? (If not, I will do an abbreviated presentation.)
- Have you looked at the sample plans? Can you give me an idea of a place to start? (I usually highlight the rates on the side with inflation for the employee and spouse/partner.)

At this point, the employee usually points to one of the plans. I immediately say "Great – that would be $____ a month. Do you realize if you paid this premium for 30 years, you would pay $_____ and your daily or monthly benefit in 30 years will be $____ and your benefit pool will be $_____?"

I use 30 years if the inflation benefit is a 5% factor. Since 5% doubles every 15 years, I can instantly calculate a 5% compound 2X or 5% compound no max without thinking hard about it. If I were using the inflation strategy of higher monthly benefits with 3% compound, I would use 24 years as my time frame. Here is an example of what I would say if the plan starts off at $7500 a month and a three year benefit period.

"Great – that would be $____ a month. That starts you off with $7500 a month which is a benefit pool of $270,000. $7500 x 36 months – do you see that? Do you realize if you paid this premium for 24 years, you would pay $____ and your monthly benefit in 24 years will be $15,000 and your benefit pool will be $540,000? And you don't have to, but if you and your spouse (partner) took the same plan, you would have over a $1,000,000 in potential benefits in 24 years?"

Or if the employee isn't sure and the person is young, perhaps under 45, I'll point to the Diamond plan and do this math for that one. For older employees, I will do it with either the Silver or Gold based on what I know so far about affordability. Their reaction lets me know if we need to drop back to Bronze or even a lower plan. If it is a struggle for them to take the same plan, I can suggest that one spouse consider a smaller plan based on what they told me about longevity and/or Alzheimer's.

Or if one of them already has a plan, we could do a smaller plan for that spouse, as I rarely recommend replacement.

Tip: if you think the spouse/partner is insurable, always talk about the premium as one monthly amount, not two, because for them it's one check, or in this case, one payroll deduction amount.

Once you've established an affordable premium, you can mention the options like restoration of benefits, survivor and shared care. This is why it's nice if the employee (and spouse/partner if he or she is there) can sit next to you and see your screen. That helps them to make a decision quickly.

When we first starting doing personal consultations, we thought most people would want to fill out the application during this time, but we have learned that most people just want our help with the benefit selection. They usually do the application on their own. If we are doing paper apps, I will walk them through it quickly, highlighting the difference between the employee app and the spouse or other family member app. If they have decided on a plan, I will check the boxes so they don't have to do it. It's really helpful to use the small "sign here" stickers that you can buy at any office supply store and put them at each signature block.

The online application for the employee is usually an easy process so sometimes the employee may want you to go ahead and get that done if you have internet access. It's not unusual, however, for even large carriers to make the spouse/family member application downloadable so they still have to be filled out and mailed in. If that's the case, we have a supply of these paper apps at the personal consultations so we can walk the employee through it so it doesn't seem intimidating.

I can't stress enough how important it is to let them know that the spouse or other family member will get an underwriting telephone call. Otherwise, your staff will wind up spending a lot of time chasing the family member down to get them to accept the phone call, and without the phone call, the application can't be processed.

OTHER IMPORTANT TIPS:

Tip #1: Make sure you are clear about the carrier's right to implement a rate increase on a class basis. If the carrier has never had a rate increase or has never had a rate increase on the group block of business, it's ok to say that as long as you immediately follow it with a statement that the carrier has the right to implement a class rate increase at some point in the future. If you think the employee is a candidate for an accelerated payment plan, you can offer that as an option. Just be sure they understand that a class rate increase is still possible during the premium paying years.

I'm making a big deal about this because we have sustained a fair amount of criticism as an industry because consumers think we told them the rates could never change. I don't think most producers have told consumers that, but not mentioning that the rates can go up can be "heard" by a consumer that they can't ever go up. Most people have heard that the Federal program had a rate increase for those who wanted to keep the automatic annual compound inflation benefit, and there are Federal employees saying they were told the rates would never change. I know we didn't tell them that in the employee education meetings, but this backlash has made me be even more careful about making sure this statement is heard loud and clear.

If part of the application is the Personal Worksheet, you have the perfect opportunity to handle this with a little humor. If the carrier has never had a rate increase it will be stated on the first page of that form in the rate increase section if you want to point it out. Then you can say:

"There are a few questions here about your financial situation that are non-invasive, but you can choose whether or not to answer them. It's a government form and it's the regulators' way of making sure we don't sell long-term care insurance to the homeless ☺ Regardless of your decision about answering the questions, I do need you to sign here, however, that I told you the rates can increase on a class basis."

Then you get their signature. If you are dealing with younger people with few assets or you are doing a large volume of personal consultations, we generally allow them to refuse to provide the information, but we definitely make sure they see the class rate increase statement as that is the primary reason they sign that form.

Tip #2: Make sure they have your email and telephone contact information if they have questions after they leave. You can offer to do a telephone consultation for a spouse or any other family member who wasn't able to attend the session with you.

Tip #3: Don't let them leave without emphasizing the open enrollment dates and encouraging them to spread the word about the one-time opportunity for limited health questions [or guaranteed acceptance] to the other employees in their department. We've had supervisors have their entire department sign up for a personal consultation. These employees will come in and say "I'm not sure what this is about, but my supervisor said I should talk to you." Then most of them enroll after hearing the education, and we would have never been in front of them otherwise.

FREQUENTLY ASKED QUESTIONS ABOUT PERSONAL CONSULTATIONS

Q. How long should you allow for each consultation?

A. This depends on the volume and the level of education. For higher education enrollments, we typically do 45 minutes. Really educated people will have more questions and need more help with the decision making process. For other types of employees or if you are enrolling a large group, you can do 30 minute time slots, but never shorter. There is too much to cover.

Q. How do you find enrollers?

A. Be careful here and don't assume that enrollers who do other products can do long-term care insurance. People with long-term care insurance experience are your best bets. Having recruited and trained long-term care insurance teams for a variety of projects, it definitely takes a certain type of person to do this product. On the Federal team, for example, I deliberately chose five people without a long-term care insurance background, thinking the diversity would be good for the team. I selected a few with a military background, one with a long-term care provider background and one who had worked in the senior health insurance counseling program in her state. None of them made the final cut unfortunately. The long-term care insurance experience was too important and couldn't be taught in just a few days.

An excellent candidate for this type of position can be a long-term care insurance producer who wants to learn worksite LTCI or someone with an employee benefits background who wants to learn long-term care insurance. Since this person is taking applications, he or she needs to have the appropriate insurance license to sell long-term care insurance and satisfy the appropriate training requirements. Our course at www.LTCiTraining.com provides an excellent foundation.

Q. How do you pay them?

A. Two ways – per diem or put them on the credit line. You may not want them on the credit line if you want to reserve the renewal compensation for your organization as you will be servicing the account. Another advantage of per diem is that you may want them to be able to say the amount of insurance someone buys doesn't affect what they get paid. If you use a per diem, geographical region will influence this, of course, but a per diem rate of $250 plus expenses is reasonable in the southeast.

Q. Can you explain how the online registration process works for personal consultations?

A. You can hire a programmer to set this up for you. A good freelance programmer will cost about $65 an hour but it is so worth it to make it easy for employees to sign up for these slots. Here is an example of the home page of the website we use for the personal consultation signup. It has the logo of the employer, the employee meeting schedule, and the ability to click on each date for which consultations are available.

The page with the time slots looks like this. There can be several columns of time slots, depending on how many consultants you have hired to do the personal consultations. On a group with several thousand employees, we kept several consultants busy for three weeks. Due to the volume, we did 30 minute slots and each consultant did 15 sessions per day.

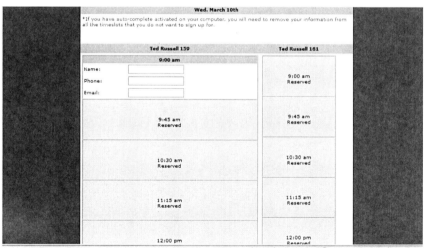

There is an admin function as well so you can see the name and contact information and make changes if people need to make changes. You should also ask your programmer to build in a confirmation email that automatically goes to each person who makes a reservation. It can look like this:

Thank you for reserving your time slot for a personal consultation to answer your questions about a long-term care insurance plan. It is a very important decision and we want to help you as much as possible. You are confirmed for [*day of week*], [*date*] and [*time*] in [*conference room location description*]. As a courtesy to others who may wish this time slot, please email [*your staff person's email address*] if you need to reschedule for any reason or call [*your phone number*] toll-free. We look forward to seeing you at your appointed time.

You have supplied the following information for the time slot:
Name:
Email:
Phone:
Date: day of week and date
Time:
Location:

CHAPTER EIGHT

You Hooked the Smallest Fish in the Pond – Now What?

Every fisherman loves to catch the really big fish, but when they look for fish to feed their family, they don't go after the big ones. In fact, any catfish connoisseur will tell you that anything over four pounds is not tender.

Sometimes the really small fish are the best, and the same goes for worksite long-term care insurance sales. And just like fishing, going after the small fish means you can catch a lot more!

Most of you will be selling in the small business market. How do I know this? Because this chart of employers by size from the Census Bureau is an eye opener: [35]

number of employees	number of firms with employees
0-4	3,670,028
5-9	1,060,787
10-19	646,816
< 20	5,377,631
20-99	535,865
100-499	90,560
< 500	6,004,056
500 +	18,071
Total	**6,022,127**

You can see that 98% of the employers in the United States have fewer than 100 employees. There are 150 million employees in the United States and less than 3 million worksite LTCI policies/certificates inforce that we know about. We can't track all of the individual policies that have been sold in the workplace, but that's a close estimate. You may be fortunate enough to participate in some of the really large firms, but since there aren't that many elephants to hunt, I want to do my best to outfit you to sell to the smaller business market. Actually, you may wind up finding a niche in the micro-business market as it is possible to get underwriting concessions down to 3 lives for employer-funded plans.

Some of the most lucrative prospects are small family-owned firms who want the business to pay their premium. If the company is a C-corporation, the company can pay the entire premium for owners and spouses and this is true for a limited pay plan of at least ten years. Further, the small business owner who owns a C-Corporation can deduct the premium for a plan with a return of premium benefit (with or without claims) and pass the money to the family tax-free. (The business owner can check with his or her corporate accountant to see if the return of premium rider should be paid with personal money to be sure the benefits are tax-free.)

You can get to these micro-business owners much faster than the large corporations. You know many of them. You see them in civic groups, chamber of commerce functions, your church or synagogue, or you work with professionals like accountants, attorneys, bankers or financial planners who advise them.

PROSPECTING LANGUAGE

All you have to do is tell everyone you know that you have come to understand that extended care at home or in a facility due to an accident or disabling event like a stroke is the greatest risk to our financial stability so you are doing your best to help everyone you know plan ahead for it. You won't have to mention it to all that many people before you get a bite on your hook because so many people are dealing with long-term care today.

UNDERWRITING

You won't get guaranteed issue on these tiny cases, but simplified underwriting is certainly possible and still a gift, especially if none of the questions deal with the height and weight ratio. Most worksite LTCI carriers require seven to ten employees who can say "no" to the short list of health questions, but it is possible to get simplified underwriting and a premium discount on an employer-paid case as small as three employees. The employer contribution can be as small as $10 per month per employee. It's also possible to get simplified underwriting for spouses with a few carriers if the employer contributes to the spouse premium. At least one company will do simplified underwriting for spouses who work full-time with no employer contribution. The smallest size for guaranteed issue is 15 employer-paid policies or for voluntary, the greater of 10% or 15 lives.[36]

Some carriers won't reduce the commission on a multi-life case but even if they do, it's not much, maybe 5% or so.

The best thing about the micro-market is that you can get a decision much faster than with a large employer prospect, and you have a much better chance of getting the spouse and other family members, especially in a family-owned company. But what I don't want you to overlook or minimize is the employee education process. Even a firm with only ten employees will still require the announcement letter and seven educational emails to get the best enrollment if it is a 100% voluntary group.

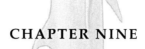

CHAPTER NINE

You Hooked Moby Dick – Now What?

First, you take a deep breath and blow into a bag.

I do know the feeling of landing a really large account, and I've already shared it with you. When I understood that I had just agreed to provide 2,000 employee meetings in four-and-a-half months, I still remember that exact feeling of the bottom falling out of my stomach. It literally took my breath away. I went in to tell our VP of Marketing and VP of Operations about it, and I remember my mouth opening and closing at least three times before sound came out. They were staring at me with concerned looks on their faces, until I was able to tell them what had just happened. Then I was able to stare at them with horrified looks on their faces.

But what a great experience!

I think as an industry we all learned tremendously from the largest long-term insurance care enrollment in the world, and the really exciting result is how much the insurance carriers have learned since then. There's still not that many in the true group market but let's applaud the ones that are there and encourage them in their efforts to cover as many employees as possible in these large firms.

You read the testimonial from Kim Maginn in the Introduction to this book and since she is out there swimming with the whales, I thought my readers would enjoy a short interview with her.

PS: Kim, what is it you do exactly that takes you into such deep waters?

Kim: I work for a six year old firm that manages voluntary insurance benefits for companies that are on the Fortune 1000 list. It takes a lot of work off the HR staff, and the insurance companies who manufacture the products love it because someone is actually pushing their products out to the employees. There are four regional reps and they pull me in to talk about group long-term care insurance.

PS: How do you get the employer's attention when you meet with them?

Kim: One of the first things I tell them is "You are a target for long-term care insurance if the average age of your employees is over 40 and the average income is over $50,000."

PS: I like the word "target". It reinforces that if they don't offer it, that employer is a target for all the productivity issues that go along with a labor force that has to handle caregiving without help.

Kim: That's right. Long-term care insurance provides both financial help and also help with finding caregivers through the free care coordination services that the major carriers offer.

PS: So are you marketing a particular company?

Kim: No. I do a Request for Proposal and send it to the large group LTCI carriers. Then I analyze the data and make a recommendation. It saves the employer a lot of time.

PS: You told me that your average client size is 15,000 employees and that you have sold 17 of these large group plans over the last couple of years. What kind of participation rates are you getting?

Kim: Anywhere from 3% to 8%, and the average is 5%.

PS: And do you accept any group? Or do you have requirements that an employer must meet?

Kim: I definitely have requirements. We never take on an employer that is just "checking a box" by offering long-term care insurance. The employer has to agree to:

1. let us and the insurance company communicate with their employees;
2. allow the use of the company's logo on the education materials;
3. an off-cycle enrollment separate from other employee benefits;
4. an open enrollment period of a minimum of four weeks, but it might go six; and
5. payroll deduction for the employee and spouse.

PS: Define "communicate with the employees" please.

Kim: The employer has to give the insurance company a mailing address file for home mailings of the announcement letter signed by a senior level executive, a personalized rate quote packet, and a reminder postcard. The employer also furnishes email addresses for eblasts.

PS: Tell us about the underwriting and is there a minimum participation requirement?

Kim: These are all guaranteed acceptance for the employees...

PS: One-time opportunity, right?

Kim: Right – for 30 to 45 days, and there is no minimum participation requirement.

PS: Online enrollment?

Kim: for the employees, yes…and the spouses and other family members are able to download an application and mail it in.

PS: What is your average premium?

Kim: $1,250

PS: Those employees must be buying inflation coverage.

Kim: 40% of them do.

PS: Of course I'm smiling about that. Do you have any idea how many spouses apply for the coverage? Or other family members?

Kim: Our spouse participation rate varies between 3% to as much as 10%. Other family members are less than the spouse participation rate.

PS: What kind of things do you look for when you make a carrier recommendation?

Kim: Well, I look at the level of employee communication they provide, of course. I also look at portability. I make sure the employees can keep the coverage for the same benefits and same premium. I also look at any pre-existing conditions clause the contract might have.

PS: You were brave enough to share your personal story about your husband's brain tumor. If you had to say one thing about what already having the long-term care insurance in place has meant to you, what would that be?

Kim: I have great peace of mind in that when the time comes that my husband and / or I will need this care, our son will not have the financial burden nor will I have to eat his cooking!! Had I not attended your training, returned home and followed through with buying long term care insurance on myself and my husband, I would be in a situation today without being able to buy it on my husband. We were in our late 30's when I purchased our policies. I bought automatic inflation and a lifetime benefit with 100% home and community based care. The premiums for both policies are under $100 month – there are many other things I would give up before letting this insurance lapse!

After the call ended, my immediate reaction was "Well, she has it made in the shade. Here she is, working for this great company and these four regional reps are bird-dogging leads for her!" But then I thought, "How many other companies out there would love to have someone just like her? The large groups they serve are asking about long-term care insurance and they have no idea where to find someone like Kim." Yes, it is very difficult to harpoon the whales, but if this is the market in which you want to be, your time would be well spent calling on the employee benefit firms in your area who work with large employers. You will have to say something intelligent fast to get their attention, so try sharing the following information.

Large employers are under pressure to offer long-term care insurance not only from employees who are asking for it, but also as a retention tool for their key employees. A recent MetLife employee benefits survey said that the top benefits objection cited by employers is retention.

Corporations who are interested in attracting, retaining and rewarding key executives now have a way to do so by increasing and protecting retirement income benefits as LTC insurance restores losses through IRS limits on qualified plans. Long-term care insurance can be the employee benefit differentiator for a progressive employer as C-Corporations can now deduct 100% of the premium for limited pay plans as an employee benefit for employees, including owners. This is an excellent way to retain key executives as neither the employer contribution nor the benefits are taxable income to the employee or the corporation owner(s).[37]

119

I had a call from an employee recently from one of my first group cases. She was 34 when her policy was issued. The premium is 100% employer paid and with the economy, the president asked her to call me and see if they could save some money by lowering their benefits. Like Kim and her husband, they all had unlimited benefit periods and 5% compound inflation for life at phenomenally low premiums, compared to today's premium. By the time I finished telling her how what they have doesn't exist anymore and that it would be impossible to replace, she said "I'm going back to the president on this. We have to find another way to save money. I'm never giving up this policy, and if I have to pay for it myself, I will."

Whether you are dealing with a large or small employer, the message to the employees is the same. This is *lifestyle insurance*, because not only will the insurance provide money to hire help, but the insurance companies will help find qualified help. People are people, no matter the size of the employer who issues the paychecks. The key is to only work with employers who will not only allow the essential employee communication process but will actively promote it because they understand the need. The really good news is that with so many people going through long-term care today, that internal champion is getting easier to find.

CHAPTER TEN

ARE YOU A RAINMAKER OR A BUILDER?

Now that you've read through the process, I can imagine some of you saying,

"WHAT is she smokin' ?? There's no way on God's green earth that I have that much time to devote to selling long-term care insurance in the workplace!! I mean, I believe in the mission and all that, but my plate is FULL with the other products I'm selling..."

Good for you to believe and to want to do something and good for you that you have a busy practice.

Don't despair.

You can still play an active role in the worksite LTCI market AND add to your bottom line with very little effort. You just have to decide that you are a RAINMAKER, not a BUILDER.

Since you have a busy practice, that means you have all kinds of connections. You may have good group prospects for a voluntary enrollment for all employees or some that are prospects just for the owners and executives or some just for the owners. You may belong to civic organizations or a church or synagogue in your community that brings you into contact with these types of prospects. You likely have close relationships with other professionals such as accountants, attorneys, your banker, and perhaps fee-based financial planners.

Or you may just know somebody who knows somebody. That's all networking is, anyway.

All you have to do is talk about the problem of caregiving. Ask a couple of questions about a long-term care event in the family – who is paying for it, and how is it affecting the primary caregiver? Many times, that's all it takes for someone to open up and start talking about a personal situation. Then you can say something like,

"You know, I read this book that talks about the right time to plan ahead for that kind of situation is really while people are working. I know a woman (or man) who specializes in making it easy for a company to offer long-term care insurance to its employees, and this person can explain all the tax incentives plus educate your employees about why it is so important to plan ahead. That way, they don't get in the same situation you've described and have to take off work to deal with it."

Then you bring in a long-term care insurance specialist you have established a relationship with. Or, if you do want to go the extra step, you become comfortable with a seven point door opener presentation. Two reasons you might want to take time to learn this extra step:

1) to solidify the referral so when you do hand it off, it is REAL; and
2) it can earn you a greater share of the commission when you negotiate the commission split if you have already half-way sold the employer.

One of my employees had a 30 year old husband who lived two years with a brain tumor then died. She had no one to leave him with and had a really tough time holding on to her job during this awful time.

Here are the salient points of the door-opener presentation:

1. Long-term care happens to people of all ages and can quickly take an employee out of work whether the employee is the care recipient or the caregiver. Anybody can be hit by a drunk driver or experience another kind of disabling accident or condition like a brain tumor, stroke or MS.

2. Long-term care can be the biggest threat to productivity in this century since workers in their caregiving years are the fastest growing segment of the labor force.

3. The impact of caregiving on productivity is HUGE:
   a) workday interruptions to handle medical visits and phone calls
   b) increased absenteeism and leaves from work
   c) decreased motivation and morale
   d) increased ongoing stress which can eventually lead to

health problems for the caregiver, which ultimately leads to more claims on your health insurance, resulting in higher health insurance premiums when this happens to enough of your employees

e) decisions to ask for part-time work or resign altogether which increases replacement costs

4. LTC insurance provides the money for your employees to hire help so they don't have to bear the entire caregiving burden without help. This means they can KEEP THEIR JOBS – the bottom line benefit for any employer.

5. The tax incentives are on the side of the employer if you want to offer an extremely meaningful benefit to increase retention of your key executives by providing a 10-pay long-term care insurance plan for the executive and his or her spouse. **It's especially important to provide it for the spouse because the executive will quickly turn into a caregiver and need time off if something happens to the spouse.**

6. As more of your competitors for executive talent are doing this, it can put you at a disadvantage not to be providing long-term care insurance as an executive benefit.

7. If you're not sure of the interest level of your employees or executives, I can email you a short employee survey so you will know one way or the other (or Susan or Dan LTCI Specialist can provide you with a short employee survey so you will know one way or the other).

And that's it – not difficult!

CHAPTER ELEVEN

WHAT'S IN YOUR "CLOSE" CLOSET?

CLOSING ON THE EMPLOYER LEVEL

I finished the Quick Payback slide recently and the Human Resources Director said something to the effect of "You coulda started with that slide and we'd have been done a lot quicker" and the CFO was nodding his head in agreement. It IS an extremely powerful slide for both the employer *and* the employee to see. The biggest objection I hear is "what if we never need it?" That slide makes that go away because it illustrates in a few seconds that the premium is so small compared to the benefit, and leaves the impression of "So what if I never need it? I spent a few dollars to have terrific peace of mind!"

So that's a financial close, but don't underestimate the "family close" and that is simply to talk about long-term care insurance as what most of us need today to take care of our families. Employer decision makers have families. Don't ever forget that when you are doing an employer presentation.

The tax incentive of being able to deduct an accelerated payment plan such as a 10-pay for both an executive and spouse provides a powerful incentive to help retain key executives.

Consider this quote from a Society for Human Resource Management report:

> From the employer's point of view, offering long-term care insurance as a voluntary benefit is a relatively low cost way to send a powerful message to employees that the organization cares about them and their future security It can be a good attraction and retention tool. 'If your competitors for talent already offer long-term care insurance, chances are good your employees know that.' [38]

Employers who ignore the tidal wave of caregiving that is just a few years away are going to suffer enormous productivity loss. Say it until you sound like a broken record: "Long-term care insurance is PRODUCTIVITY INSURANCE for the employer and LIFESTYLE INSURANCE for the employee."

Don't give up on a company that you consider a good prospect until you can get them to do an employee survey. That lets the employees tell the decision makers that they want long-term care insurance, and their voices speak much louder than yours.

CLOSING ON THE EMPLOYEE LEVEL

Let's go back to the personal consultation. I work with them to get something in the ballpark for affordability and while they are thinking about it, I tell them the carrier's rules for being able to decrease benefits in the future at issue age. Usually the benefit period (or benefit account) and the daily or monthly benefit can be decreased at any point in the future but maybe it is only the daily benefit. Whatever it is, my next phrase will go something like this:

"Now, if you do take the [*highest plan they are considering*] and the premium becomes uncomfortable for any reason at any point in the future, you can always decrease the [*daily benefit*] [*benefit period*] at issue age – the age you are now, and it would lower the premium significantly. However, if you take the [*lower plan they are considering*] and then later you think 'I sure wish we had bought [*the higher plan they are considering*]', you will have to go through full underwriting and [*name of insurance company*] will charge you for the increased benefit based on your new age, not the age you are today. Plus, you risk not being able to qualify medically to increase your benefits.

You just told them the truth, didn't you? The insurance company is happy when people decrease the benefits but when a request comes in to increase benefits, the company thinks the policyholder may know something the company doesn't about the policyholder's health. An intensive underwriting process follows.

Of course the most common objection is the same as all of us have heard in the individual market for years. It's so common that I make sure it is brought up in the Q&A at the end of the employee education session if someone doesn't ask it.

But what if I never need long-term care?

"Let me ask you a question. Did you lie awake last night and worry that you haven't had enough house fires to justify your car insurance? Or have you worried that you haven't had enough automobile accidents to justify your automobile insurance premium? Because if that is something that really worries you, just tell me where you parked and I'll be glad to back into your car before I leave today. *(By now they're usually laughing a little.)* I hope you never need long-term care and if you don't, you've made a ___ a month mistake *(insert the monthly premium you've been discussing)*. But if you don't take this coverage and you do need care, then you've made at least a $5000, $10,000, $15,000 a month mistake, so which kind of mistake would you rather make? You can find [$___] a month. How hard would it be to find $15,000 a month? And remember, when you need care, the premium stops and your benefit continues to grow *(adjust the last phrase according to the inflation benefit they are considering).*

Getting the Spouse/Partner App

We have achieved a significant spouse/partner application percentage – upwards of 30%. I've heard large group carriers say at industry conferences that it is about 2% in large group enrollments. I think the main reason we have been successful in getting as many spouses covered is because **we set the expectation from the second we walk in the door that spouses will apply.** You will remember in Chapter Five, *The Blueprint of the Perfect Employer Presentation* that we make these points crystal clear:

1) The announcement letter must go to the homes (even if we have to pay the postage).
2) Each education piece says spouses and family members are welcome at the employee meetings and personal consultations.
3) We position long-term care insurance first as taking care of the family and second, as a financial product.
4) We go to great lengths to ensure the spouse can access the information with presentation CDs and/or webinars and the like.

The most important thing we do however is at the personal consultation. We ask the same questions about the spouse as we do the employee (name, age, health, longevity, Alzheimer's, etc.) and there's never a question that the spouse won't apply if he or she is insurable. We may have to spell it out and we don't hesitate. If there is a mention of the spouse not applying, I'm sure I get a horrified look on my face and say something like:

"John, you are doing this for Judy, and Judy is doing this for you. The one who needs care may not know what is going on, which means the caregiver spouse is the one who can suffer most."

The next sentence will deal with their children and grandchildren.

"And both of you are doing this to protect Bill and Amy by giving them the resources to take care of you and keep their own family life going with Janie and David. Didn't you tell me both of them really want to go to college?""

A really common objection that you will hear is this one, especially if you live near a military base:

Won't the VA pay for long-term care??

Answer: "If the VA were able to pay for long-term care, why would the government be offering long-term care insurance to the military, both active and retired? The VA only pays about 2% of long-term care, and that includes home care as well as nursing home care." [39]

What happens if I still need care after my benefits are used up?

Answer: "I always advise people to buy the benefit plan they can afford. Even if it is only a two year benefit period, that's that much time of private-pay choices that you might not otherwise have."

Additional answer if you are offering a Partnership plan: "Then you can turn to Medicaid for help and if you otherwise qualify, you will receive care without having to spend most of your assets down to get it."

CHAPTER TWELVE

THE BLOOPER CHAPTER

Make these pages your Lucky 13 chapter. Learn from my bloopers, because I've already made the big ones. Spare yourself the pain by not repeating my mistakes!

It's hard to talk about our mistakes. It's embarrassing, and we would just as soon people not know about them, right? But as difficult as this is going to be (and probably why I saved this chapter for last), I would not be completing the purpose of this book if I didn't share them with you. These were all in 2004-05, except the last one which I'm sad to say happened recently. Since most are older, I don't have consistent information on them, but I was able to dig up enough for you to see why they didn't work.

Blooper #1: employee college – 120 employees

Case description: This was the first group we did. It could have been great. We followed the process of the announcement letter to the homes and the seven emails and the employer set up one employee education meeting. It was well attended. We handed out a notebook with rate quotes for all ages for three benefit periods for three different monthly benefits plus the product brochure. That meant a total of NINE benefit options. To complicate matters further, the rate quotes showed single, married with spouse and married without spouse, so three sets of rates with each of those benefit plans. So let's see, we're now up to 27 sets of rates. We went for the association discount but not an employer program with simplified underwriting as we were afraid we couldn't meet the participation requirement.

Results: one couple bought and the husband had to be deferred for 12 months due to a health issue (good news – he was accepted when he reapplied).

Problems:
- Too many options – wow!
- Gave them rate quotes instead of putting the rates for four sample plans for all ages on one piece of paper
- One group meeting - should have had several
- No personal consultations

Blooper #2: law firm – 72 employees.
Case description: We were very excited about this one because 26 employees indicated interest on the employee survey. We did the pre-education and scheduled one meeting. We did the four sample plans with rates for all ages on a single sheet. When I arrived to do the meeting, I knew right away there was a problem because there was one attorney in attendance and the rest were clerical and staff, almost all women. We did not do personal consultations. I followed up with the broker who was going to follow up with the meeting attendees. He mentioned he had seen the attorney who owns the firm at church and mentioned the offering. The owner attorney knew nothing about it.

Results: one application from a woman who was having health issues.

Problems:
- No management support. The broker's relationship was with the HR person who was a woman with very little authority in the firm.

- Left an inexperienced broker to follow up; we didn't do personal consultations

Blooper #3: electric company – 385 employees

Case description: 45% of the employees had incomes over $40,000. However, only about 50 had post-high school education. The HR Director was difficult. She would only agree to send out 2 of the 7 educational articles and they both went out in one email, and she sent out an announcement memo to the employees but it did not go to the homes. Her argument was that she would have mandatory meetings. She prided herself on being an expert on health insurance. Yet I had to spell out in detail from the health insurance contract why the health insurance plan won't pay for long-term care. She was totally price-oriented and bought a plan on herself only, not her spouse. She bought 5% simple inflation, even though I counseled her that compound was in her best interest at her age. There were two meetings and they were well attended with a lot of questions. We used the four sample plans on one sheet and we had simplified underwriting for 30 days. We handed out applications which the employees were to turn into the HR director as she said that was their method for enrolling other products. We did not do personal consultations.

Result: Five applications – two couples and the HR director. One couple was declined for health issues

Problems:
- Low management support as the HR Director resisted our complete education process
- Education level was too low for a voluntary long-term care insurance offering, at least without the full blown pre-education effort
- I believe this could have been turned around if we had offered personal consultations, but we hadn't learned that yet.

Blooper #4: small bank with 165 employees.

Case description: 30% had salaries over $40,000; 78% of the employees were female and only 21% of those made over $40,000; 60% of employees were over age 40. HR Director couldn't have been more supportive. Our presenter who did six meetings in three locations was very well received and treated like gold. The meetings were "lunch and learn" then 6:30 – 8 p.m. for family members. We offered simplified underwriting. We offered 3 monthly benefits, 3 benefit periods, and 2 inflation options. Many expressed verbal interest. The broker who brought us the case was a wonderful door opener but wanted no involvement in the enrollment.

Result: ZERO applications!!

Problems:

- Salaries were too low
- Female content too high especially since most were in clerical, low income positions; even though they were very interested, the "ask my husband" would be enough to negate the interest especially with no personal consultations
- Low education level
- Too many benefit options
- No personal consultations
- Broker not overly involved

Blooper #5: community hospital - 1100 employees

Case Description: Only 32% made over $40,000; 72% over age 40. The HR Director was very difficult. She left the initial employer presentation early. She wouldn't participate in the payroll call or employee education strategy session. She later wanted the enrollment website shut down so that no one could apply after the open enrollment period, even though it was full underwriting. We won that battle to keep it open, then she pulled the payroll deduction opportunity. She didn't want the logo used on any education materials after signing a consent form to allow it to be used. She wouldn't provide more than one private conference room for the employee education. She didn't want the seven educational emails sent out. You might wonder why this case even got off the ground. It was brought to us by the benefits consulting firm who has had this account over 35 years, the owner of which was a personal friend of mine. He needed help and I wanted to do what I could. It was a mistake I will try very hard not to repeat. It turned out to be a "check the box" enrollment which we realized after the master application had been signed.

Result: 11 applications

Problems:

- income too low
- didn't follow the pre-education recommendations
- payroll deduction was shut down
- the consultant didn't want to risk the relationship by being firm about what we needed to do for a successful enrollment

A close call: We did another private college with 400 employees which was a near-blooper. The college is in a poorer part of the state that had been hit hard with unemployment but a very family-oriented area. Everything was going perfectly – great HR person, perfect pre-education process with simplified underwriting, 67 people attended meetings. We did about 20 personal consultations, half of which included the spouse. After the last personal consultation, the HR director got a phone call that the health insurance was going up 25% and he had to tell the employees before the end of the open enrollment. The outcome was 42 applications (78% with compound inflation; average premium $1,190) but I know it would have been many more without that announcement.

135

So let's do a post-mortem. What did we learn from these cases?

1) Management support is ESSENTIAL. Without a supportive HR person whom I refer to as the internal champion, success is nearly always elusive.
2) the pre-education process must be followed
3) the plans must be presented very simply and no more than four sample plans
4) education level is important
5) high female workforce is detrimental
4) personal consultations maximize participation

Here is the overall learning for me, no matter how favorable the above components are:

Poor people can't afford the premium unless someone else is paying the bill.

And at some level, is it kind to educate thoroughly, get low –income employees so excited that they think they must have it, then show them premiums that are out of reach for most of them? So now I can hear some of you coming back with the age-old argument "But isn't something better than nothing?" Here are a couple of points of discussion that I will leave you with on this point:

1. if the daily or monthly benefit is too low at claim time and the family can't make up the difference between what the insurance benefit pays and the charge, they will spend down quickly and the insured will have to turn to Medicaid quickly; and
2. if you are offering a Partnership plan and the employees don't buy the state-required inflation benefit for their age, they won't receive the asset protection when they apply for Medicaid.

When one goes on Medicaid, Medicaid pays what is left over after the insurance benefit and the person's income pays. So the "something is better than nothing" is good for the economy as even small benefits mean that much less for Medicaid to pay. I'm not sure the employees and their families will see it that way when they find out their benefit is too small to keep them off Medicaid for even a short time.

But let's end this chapter on a positive note!

Several years ago we helped a housing authority in one of the poorer parts of our beautiful state. This is an organization that helps low-income families find housing. The employees are also low-income for the most part. Imagine my surprise when their health insurance broker called me to say they wanted a 100% employer paid program!

It turned out that the 55 year old program director had been through a long-term care situation with a close family member and saw up close and personal how important long-term care insurance can be to a family. She authorized the premium to be paid in full for all the employees to have a four year benefit period, $4500 monthly benefit for all types of care, 5% compound 2X inflation and a 90 day calendar day waiting period. We were able to do simplified underwriting with four questions. These employees didn't have access to email, so the process was different for this one.

The program director sent the announcement letter, then we had all the employees come in at 7 a.m. so I could do a short slide presentation about what they were getting and tell them what a GIFT this benefit is from their employer. I had stripped the apps down to the essential pages and already filled out everything except their personal information and their answers to the health questions. We had "school" and everyone completed the apps at the same time and signed in the appropriate places. I walked around and checked their papers, then had 27 applications to take with me. We gave them applications to take home to their spouses and we received several spouse and family apps over the next few weeks. That case is in its fourth year now. I smile every time I think about it because it was such a privilege to be able to participate in providing these employees with something that is going to add so much dignity to their lives in an economically depressed area of our state.

SUMMARY

We've all heard, read and many have felt the effects of the economic downturn on sales in general. Well, I hope this book has made it abundantly clear that **there is no reason for your LTCI sales to be down** – even in this economy! If you are not spending some portion of your time developing the piece of the LTCI market that represents half of all LTCI sales, you need to retool your business plan for the rest of this year and forward.

And see, I told you it wasn't all that complicated. Why am I telling you all this? It's quite simple, really. For the past 22 years I have made it my personal mission in life to promote the benefits of long-term care insurance...to the point of describing myself as "a consumer advocate for long-term care insurance". (You are welcome and encouraged to use that title as well.) In that time my organization has trained over 65,000 insurance professionals with one ultimate goal. I want American families to benefit by having meaningful long term care services when needed, and I want our long-term care insurance industry to prosper. They are not mutually exclusive. But in order to prosper, we all need to place a focus on worksite LTCI. It's where the market has gone and this book has shown you exactly how to get there. Will you be a part of it? I truly hope so – for all of us as producers, but mostly for the families who trust us to take care of them.

SOURCES

1. "Multi-Life in the Large Group Market", Session 09-19, 9th Annual ILTCI Conference, Reno, NV, 3/30/09
2. I say almost 20 years because long-term care insurance policies have been good since about 1991 when the old restrictions were removed like requiring a prior hospital stay, requiring skilled care first, and so forth.
3. 2008 NAIC LTCI Experience Reports
4. 18 is the youngest age one can buy LTCI in the United States
5. *LTC Consultants' carrier survey 12/08*
6. LIMRA, *Long-Term Care Insurance Sales Supplements,* ongoing (received 3/10)
7. TIAA-Cref Press Release, "The Current State of Americans' Retirement Plans", January 8, 2010)
8. Savage, Terry. *Chicago Sun-Times* Financial Columnist, author of *"The New Savage Number: How Much Money Do You Need To Retire?"* John Wiley & Sons, 2009, p. 218
9. Multiple LTCI Carrier Cost of Care Surveys, 2009
10. *2009 Making Sense of Investor Needs in the Retirement Income Market,* Financial Research Corporation, Boston, Mass. (www.frcnet.com)
11. Agency for Healthcare Research and Quality for 1987 info and carrier cost surveys for 2009
12. Centers for Disease Control and Prevention, 12/31/08
13. "Multi-Life in the Large Group Market", Session 09-19, 9th Annual ILTCI Conference, Reno, NV, 3/30/09
14. MetLife 8th Annual Study of Employee Benefits Trends: Findings from the National Survey of Employers and Employees, 2010, p. 35
15. Shelton, Phyllis. **Long-Term Care: Your Financial Planning Guide**, LTCi Publishing, Inc., 2008, pp. 1,2
16. "Who Buys Long-Term Care Insurance? A 15-Year Study of Buyers and Non-Buyers, 1990-2005", America's Health Insurance Plans, April 2007

17. This is an annual long-term care insurance conference that grew out of the Society of Actuaries long-term care insurance track. The 2010 conference was held March 14-17 in New Orleans, Louisiana.

18. Bureau of Labor Statistics Data from National Compensation Survey: Employee Benefits in the United States, March 2009, http://www.bls.gov/ncs/ebs/benefits/2009/ebbl0044.pdf

19. "Statistics of U.S. Businesses", Census Bureau, "Number of Firms. . . by Employment Size...for US and States", http://www2.census.gov/econ/susb/data/2006/us_state_totals_2006.xls (The first tables containing **2007 data** will be available by June 2010.)

20. LIMRA, 2010

21. "Employment Projections 2008-2018", Bureau of Labor Statistics, 12/10/09

22. LIMRA, *Long-Term Care Insurance Sales Supplements,* ongoing (received 3/10)

23. LTC Partnership Reports for California, Connecticut, Indiana and New York as of 9/30/09

24. "Caregiving in the U.S. 2009", National Alliance for Caregiving in Collaboration with AARP, funded by MetLife Foundation, November 2009, p. 4

25. Kaye, H. Stephen, Charlene Harrington, and Mitchell P. LaPlante. "Long-Term Care: Who Gets It, Who Provides It, Who Pays, and How Much?" *Health Affairs,* January 2010 29:1, p. 13.

26. *Ibid*

27. Based on an average 6% compound growth rate between $56 daily cost in 1987 compared to $198 in 2009. Source for 1987 costs: Medical Expenditure Panel Survey (MEPS) Chartbook #6 "Nursing Home Expenses 1987-1996", Agency for Research and Quality, p. 6. Source for 2009 cost of care: MetLife Cost of Care Survey, October 2009.

28. Kaye, H. Stephen, Charlene Harrington, and Mitchell P. LaPlante. "Long-Term Care: Who Gets It, Who Provides It, Who Pays, and How Much?" *Health Affairs,* January 2010 29:1, p. 17.

29. Kemper et al. "Long-term Care Over an Uncertain Future: What Can Current Retirees Expect?" *Inquiry* 42: Winter 2005/2006, p. 342.

30. "Employment Projections 2008-2018", Bureau of Labor Statistics, 12/10/09

31. "Caregiving in the U.S. 2009", National Alliance for Caregiving/AARP, November 2009, p. 4

32. "Table 1. Civilian labor force by age, sex, race, and Hispanic origin, 1998, 2008, and projected 2018", Bureau of Labor Statistics Economic News Release, last modified December 11, 2009.

33. "The Growth in Employer-Sponsored LTCI", Center for Insurance Education, America's Health Insurance Plans, July 30, 2008

34. Chandler, Michael A. "When A Kid Becomes the Caregiver", *Washington Post.com*, April 25, 2007, A01 .

35. "Statistics of U.S. Businesses", Census Bureau, "Number of Firms. . . by Employment Size...for US and States", http://www2.census.gov/econ/susb/data/2006/us_state_totals_2006.xls (The first tables containing **2007 data** will be available by June 2010.)

36. *LTC Consultants* online LTCI Policy Comparison and discussions with Bill Comfort, Jr. about MetLife and John Noble, Director, LTC Benefits, Unum, and Bob Nardone, Regional Sales Director, MedAmerica.

37. *Sixth Annual Study of Employee Benefit Trends*, MetLife, March 2008, p. 25

38. Sammer, Joanne. "Planning for the Future: Long-Term Care as an Employee Benefit", Society of Human Resource Managers Library, October 2008. Quote by Jennifer Loftus, National Director, Astron Solutions, HR consulting firm based in New York.

39. 2008 National Health Expenditures, Centers for Medicare and Medicaid Services, released January 2010.

TAX INCENTIVES FOR LONG-TERM CARE INSURANCE

Let's dig a little deeper into the tax incentives.

An age-based amount of long-term insurance premium counts as a medical expense per IRC S213(d)(10)(A). Since medical expenses in excess of 7 1/2% are tax deductible, this means that a portion of your long-term care insurance premium will help you reach that threshold and may even put you over it to receive a tax deduction. Here are the amounts that count for 2010, and they are allowed to increase each year based on the Medical Consumer Price Index:

Attained age before the close of the taxable year	Amount that counts as an allowable medical expense
40 and younger	$330
41-50	$620
51-60	$1,230
61-70	$3,290
71 and older	$4,110.00

- LTC insurance premium up to the above limits is treated like health insurance for the self-employed tax deduction. ["Self-employed" means sole proprietorships, partnerships, "greater than 2% shareholders" of S-Corporations or Limited Liability

Corporations.] For example, my health insurance costs $4,500 a year. My LTC insurance policy is $1,400 of which $1,230 can be applied based on the above table to give me a total premium of $5,730 for 2010. Therefore, my adjusted gross income will be lowered by $5,730 for the 2010 tax year. (This means absolutely no excuses for not having a LTC insurance policy if you are an insurable self-employed insurance agent!) Note: Spousal premium of a "greater than 2% shareholder" is treated the same way if the business pays the premium for the spouse, even if the spouse is an employee of the company.

EMPLOYER/EMPLOYEE

• Premium contributions made by employers are not taxable income to employees. [IRC Sec. 106(a)]

• Benefits are tax-free to employees, whether or not the employer contributed to the premium. [IRC Secs. 104(a)(3), 105(b)] (This is an advantage LTC insurance has over disability income insurance.)

• Employers will receive a tax deduction for any portion of long-term care insurance premiums paid for employees and spouses. [IRC 7702B(a)(3) and Sec. 162] (Important: Employers who are considered self-employed [sole proprietors, partnerships, "greater than 2% shareholders" of S-Corporations or Limited Liability Corporations] may deduct only LTCI premium paid for employees. If the business pays the self-employed owner's premium, the premium is taxable income to the self-employed owner. The age-based amount of premium is deductible as part of the self-employed health insurance deduction, and any remaining premium is deductible as salary.

• LTC insurance premium is not a deductible business expense for sole proprietors and single-member LLC's, but they do get the self-employed health insurance deduction explained above. The premium is not taxable income since these individuals do not take a salary per se.

- However, an individual who is both self-employed and an employee eligible to participate in an employer-subsidized plan maintained by his employer or his spouse's employer cannot take the deduction. [Code Sec. 7702B(c), 7702B(b), Code Sec. 162(l)(2)(B).]

- 100% of LTC premium contributions are tax deductible to a C-Corporation on behalf of all employees, spouses, and bona fide dependents per the IRS, regardless of ownership in the company. [IRC 162(a), IRC 162(l) 162(l)(2)(C), 213(d)]

- Employers can select by class (e.g. tenure, job title, salary) as long as it is not a self-insured LTC plan, which is rare in the marketplace; e.g. CalPERS (California Public Employee's Retirement System), the Virginia Retirement System and Hewlett-Packard.

- LTC insurance cannot be included in a cafeteria plan under Section 125, nor can LTC services be reimbursed by a Flexible Spending Account. (The only exception to this is if LTCI premium is paid out of a health savings account that was funded through a Section 125 plan.)

- The purchase of a qualified long-term care insurance (LTCi) policy cannot be financed through a salary reduction arrangement for the same reason it can't be funded with pre-tax dollars from a Section 125 cafeteria plan. The tax code specifically excludes any product which is advertised, marketed, or offered as long-term care insurance from the definition of qualified benefits that can be offered through a Section 125 plan. [IRC § 7702B(a)(1). IRC § 125(f)]

- Can a single premium (10-pay, etc.) be deducted in a single year? If an individual pays the premiums, the age-based amount for the above table counts as a medical expense each year until all of the premium is accounted for. What's the answer if an employer pays the premium? The general consensus throughout the industry is that a limited pay period less than 10 years may not be viewed favorably by the IRS. But the real answer is - see a tax professional!

- If a corporation deducts the premium and is also the beneficiary of a Return of Premium upon death, the deduction for the corporation is nullified and the refund is included in the employer's gross income. (ROP at death is allowed in a tax-qualified LTCI policy but ROP due to a cancellation is included in gross income, to the extent the premium was deducted.)

- Qualified long-term care insurance premiums are eligible expenses in a Section 105 Medical Reimbursement Plan, which is available to small businesses and farms to deduct family health insurance premiums and medical, vision and dental expenses not covered by insurance. To be eligible, a sole proprietor must be married and be legitimately able to employ his/her spouse.

- The age-based LTC insurance premiums are an acceptable medical expense under a Health Reimbursement Arrangement, the employer-provided medical care expense plan in which reimbursements for medical care expenses made from the plan are excludable from employee gross income. [Rev. Rul. 2002-41]

HEALTH SAVINGS ACCOUNTS

Section 1201 of the Medicare Drug Bill, Public Law No. 108-173, added Section 223 to the Internal Revenue Code to permit eligible individuals to establish Health Savings Accounts (HSA's) for taxable years beginning with 2004. Health Savings Accounts are available to anyone with a deductible of at least $1,200 with a maximum contribution of $3,050 for an individual plan with annual out-of-pocket expenses (deductibles, co-payments, not premiums) not exceeding $5,950 (Family plans: at least a $2,400 deductible with a maximum contribution of $6,150 and out-of-pocket max of $11,900). See www.irs.gov for updates each January.

Any unused amounts at the end of the year in HSA's are allowed to grow tax-deferred, which is much better than the "use it or lose it" feature of a flexible spending account.

Americans who have high-deductible health insurance plans (HDHPs) in the amounts specified above may deposit up to the maximum contribution above (from 2007 on) in a pre-tax account and may use that money to pay for any IRS-approved medical expense, plus three types of insurance premium: COBRA premium, health insurance premium only if the applicant is receiving unemployment, and "qualified" long-term care insurance premium, which means the age-based amounts. Also as of 2007, it is no longer necessary to contribute throughout the year. For example, if one is eligible in December, he or she can contribute the entire allowed amount for the entire year.

In addition, individuals over 65 may use HSA dollars to pay premiums for Medicare Part A or B, Medicare HMO, premium for employer-sponsored health insurance (including retiree health insurance), but not Medicare supplement premiums. (Note: Americans who are eligible for Medicare can't set up a Health Savings Account, but if they set one up prior to becoming eligible for Medicare, they can keep it – they just can't make new contributions after becoming Medicare-eligible.) They also can continue to pay long-term care insurance premium with HSA dollars after turning 65.

THE
CLASS ACT

Does the word "whitewash" come to mind?

THE CLASS ACT (YES, YOU STILL NEED LONG-TERM CARE INSURANCE!!)

The Community Living Assistance Services and Supports (CLASS) Act is a provision in the new health care reform bill (Public Law 111-148) that is supposed to provide a small cash benefit of $50 - $75 a day with a lifetime benefit period depending on the level of impairment (needing help with 2 Activities of Daily Living vs. 4 ADLs). The anticipated implementation year is 2013, and all employees will pay through payroll deduction unless they opt out. Premium must be paid for at least five years before benefits can be claimed. Earlier discussions of this legislation suggested low monthly premiums such as $40 a month. The final version says in Sec. 3203 that the premium is yet to be determined and that it will be based on keeping the program solvent throughout a 75 year period. Premiums can start as low as $5 a month for people below poverty level and workers who are also full-time students under age 22. People who drop out for more than 90 days will have to re-enter at attained age. Even so, the premium can be recalculated in the future and rate increases applied except to enrollees who are age 65 and have paid premium for at least 20 years.

The concern about this program is two-fold: that it will cost much more than is projected and that it will lull Americans into a false sense of security that they are truly protected for long-term care. A $50-$75 a day benefit seems very small vs. current costs of $150+ per day for 8 hours of home care, the cost of which could triple in the next 20 years due to the extreme shortage of caregivers. The inflation index for the CLASS Act daily benefit is Urban CPI, which averages around 3.5% per year. [Sec. 3205 (b) (1) (B)] Also, employers don't have to offer it and even when they do, employees can opt out per the "Alternative Enrollment Procedures" section as follows:

Sec. 3204 Enrollment and Disenrollment Requirements

(2) Alternative Enrollment Procedures - The procedures established under paragraph (1) shall provide for an alternative enrollment process for an individual described in subsection (c) in the case of such an individual--

(A) who is self-employed
(B) who has more than 1 employer; or
(C) whose employer does not elect to participate in the automatic enrollment process established by the Secretary.

Premiums will vary by age at enrollment and by year of enrollment. However, the head actuary at CMS (the government branch that runs Medicare and Medicaid) thinks that the average premium for the program should be more like $240 per month, although premiums will vary by age at enrollment and year of enrollment.* I just can't see employees accepting a high level of premium for so little benefit. We know how hard it is to educate employees to buy private long-term care insurance for much less premium than that. $15 million over the next five years was approved for what we thought would go to continue the Own Your Future program. Now it looks like those dollars may be used to provide consumer education about the CLASS Act.

Finally, a really big reason it passed is because employees are guaranteed acceptance, including employees who already need help with activities of daily living; i.e. wheelchair-bound employees. Non-working spouses do not appear to be eligible at all, but we would expect this oversight to be clarified before the program is implemented.

Because it requires premiums to be paid for the five year time period before any benefits can be paid out, Congress looked at it as a revenue generator to help fund the overall health care reform bill. I think they will be sadly disappointed when they see how few employees will accept it. The head actuary at CMS thinks the participation will be only 2%.* Most of them will likely be people who have health issues, which will drive up the number of claims, which can ultimately lead to the program being underfunded. Many believe it will fall way short of the revenue generator it is expected to be.

*Foster, Richard S. "Estimated Financial Effects of the "Patient Protection and Affordable Care Act," as amended, Department of Health and Human Services, CMS Office of the Actuary, April 22, 2010 memorandum, pp. 14,15.

You can watch my website for updates at www.ltcconsultants.com.

Sample Rate Pages

You have to adjust the plan design to get the appropriate rates
for the group.

Here are three sample rate pages with three different companies and benefit designs. We ALWAYS use them, whether it is online enrollment or not. You can customize the bottom to include messages such as:

1) how the inflation option works
2) an inflation statement if you are doing a Partnership offering
3) link for personal consultations
4) link for online enrollment

Sample A is a company that charges the same premium for someone who is part of a couple whether the spouse/partner is issued or not. The 5% compound 2X inflation option is approved in that state for Partnership applicants below age 61, so the note at the bottom shows that.

Sample B is a company that charges a different premium based on single, part of a couple but the spouse/partner isn't issued or part of a couple and the spouse/partner is issued.

Sample C is a company that charges the same for everyone, regardless of marital status.

They should be printed two-sided so it is one sheet of paper.

Again, these are sample plans. You will design your own based on your area and demographics. If you were designing a sheet just for retired employees, you would likely show a lower benefit for the Bronze plan and shift the others accordingly. Some retirees may already have a plan and just need to supplement it with the employer's new offering, so you would want a lower Bronze benefit to accommodate that.

Company A
Sample Plans With Inflation Coverage (2X Compound)*

Company Logo
Goes Here

Age	Bronze - $100,000 Policy Limit $3,000 Home Care Mo. Benefit $4,000 Facility Monthly Benefit 33 mo. HHC / 25 mo. facility		Silver - $200,000 Policy Limit $4,500 Home Care Mo. Benefit $6,000 Facility Monthly Benefit 44 mo. HHC / 33 mo. facility		Gold - $300,000 Policy Limit $4,500 Home Care Mo. Benefit $6,000 Facility Monthly Benefit 66 mo. HHC / 50 mo. facility		Diamond - $500,000 Policy Limit $4,500 Home Care Mo. Benefit $6,000 Facility Monthly Benefit 9 years HHC / 7 years facility	
	Single	Married	Single	Married	Single	Married	Single	Married
18-29	$22.57	$15.19	$39.85	$26.83	$49.56	$33.36	$59.49	$40.05
30	$23.86	$16.07	$42.20	$28.41	$52.43	$35.29	$62.96	$42.39
31	$25.16	$16.94	$44.56	$30.00	$55.66	$37.47	$66.67	$44.88
32	$26.57	$17.89	$47.26	$31.82	$58.89	$39.65	$70.74	$47.62
33	$28.10	$18.92	$49.96	$33.64	$62.48	$42.06	$74.93	$50.44
34	$29.74	$20.02	$53.02	$35.69	$66.07	$44.48	$79.36	$53.43
35	$31.51	$21.21	$56.08	$37.75	$70.02	$47.14	$84.15	$56.65
36	$33.39	$22.48	$59.49	$40.05	$74.33	$50.04	$89.30	$60.11
37	$35.50	$23.90	$63.13	$42.50	$79.00	$53.18	$94.68	$63.74
38	$37.62	$25.33	$67.01	$45.11	$83.67	$56.33	$100.55	$67.69
39	$39.85	$26.83	$71.13	$47.88	$89.06	$59.95	$106.65	$71.80
40	$42.32	$28.49	$75.59	$50.89	$94.44	$63.58	$113.24	$76.23
41	$45.03	$30.31	$80.29	$54.05	$100.55	$67.69	$120.30	$80.98
42	$47.85	$32.21	$85.35	$57.46	$106.65	$71.80	$127.84	$86.06
43	$50.79	$34.19	$90.76	$61.10	$113.48	$76.39	$135.86	$91.46
44	$54.08	$36.41	$96.52	$64.98	$120.66	$81.23	$144.36	$97.18
45	$57.61	$38.78	$102.75	$69.17	$128.56	$86.55	$153.58	$103.39
46	$61.25	$41.23	$109.45	$73.68	$136.82	$92.11	$163.39	$110.00
47	$65.25	$43.92	$116.50	$78.43	$145.44	$97.91	$173.92	$117.09
48	$69.60	$46.85	$124.26	$83.65	$155.13	$104.43	$185.18	$124.66
49	$74.18	$49.94	$132.49	$89.19	$165.55	$111.45	$197.15	$132.72
50	$79.12	$53.26	$141.31	$95.13	$176.32	$118.70	$210.07	$141.42
51	$84.41	$56.82	$150.71	$101.46	$188.17	$126.68	$223.84	$150.69
52	$90.05	$60.62	$160.83	$108.27	$200.38	$134.89	$238.44	$160.52
53	$96.17	$64.74	$171.64	$115.55	$214.02	$144.08	$254.12	$171.08
54	$102.75	$69.17	$183.40	$123.46	$228.39	$153.75	$271.00	$182.44
55	$109.80	$73.92	$195.86	$131.85	$243.83	$164.15	$289.20	$194.69
56	$118.39	$79.70	$211.26	$142.22	$262.86	$176.96	$311.34	$209.59
57	$126.62	$85.24	$225.84	$152.03	$280.82	$189.05	$332.41	$223.78
58	$135.43	$91.17	$241.71	$162.72	$300.21	$202.10	$355.03	$239.01
59	$144.95	$97.58	$258.76	$174.19	$321.39	$216.36	$379.57	$255.53
60	$156.01	$106.05	$278.39	$189.25	$345.81	$235.08	$408.06	$277.40
61	$168.47	$114.52	$300.84	$204.51	$373.46	$253.88	$440.74	$299.61
62	$180.58	$122.76	$322.36	$219.14	$400.40	$272.19	$472.34	$321.09
63	$195.15	$132.67	$348.57	$236.96	$433.07	$294.40	$510.88	$347.30
64	$210.91	$143.38	$376.79	$256.14	$468.27	$318.33	$552.65	$375.70
65	$229.01	$155.68	$409.71	$278.52	$510.28	$346.89	$603.77	$410.44
66	$249.82	$169.83	$447.33	$304.09	$557.68	$379.11	$659.91	$448.60
67	$267.57	$181.90	$479.30	$325.83	$597.90	$406.45	$707.91	$481.24
68	$286.26	$194.60	$513.16	$348.85	$640.63	$435.50	$758.90	$515.90
69	$305.90	$207.95	$548.66	$372.98	$685.52	$466.02	$812.88	$552.60
70	$326.47	$226.24	$586.17	$406.21	$733.28	$508.16	$869.86	$602.81
71	$354.92	$245.96	$637.66	$441.90	$798.64	$553.46	$948.26	$657.15
72	$377.96	$261.93	$679.63	$470.98	$852.14	$590.54	$1,012.54	$701.69
73	$401.83	$278.47	$723.24	$501.21	$907.45	$628.86	$1,079.33	$747.98
74	$426.16	$295.33	$767.45	$531.84	$963.82	$667.93	$1,146.85	$794.76
75	$534.44	$370.37	$965.54	$669.12	$1,218.43	$844.37	$1,456.75	$1,009.53

All monthly and policy limits grow 5% compounded annually until they have doubled in 15 years, as long as benefits are not exhausted.
These rates include "shared waiver" which waives the premium for both spouses when one spouse needs care.

you are offering a Partnership plan and this inflation option is approved for under age 61 in your state:
these plans qualify for dollar-for-dollar asset protection in the event the insured ever has to apply for Medicaid."]

Optional: Insert link to online registration for personal consultations and/or online enrollment.

Customized rates and plans available up to age 85 upon request

Company A
Sample Plans Without Inflation Coverage*

Company Logo
Goes Here

	Bronze - $100,000 Policy Limit $3,000 Home Care Mo. Benefit $4,000 Facility Monthly Benefit 33 mo. HHC / 25 mo. facility		Silver - $200,000 Policy Limit $4,500 Home Care Mo. Benefit $6,000 Facility Monthly Benefit 44 mo. HHC / 33 mo. facility		Gold - $300,000 Policy Limit $4,500 Home Care Mo. Benefit $6,000 Facility Monthly Benefit 66 mo. HHC / 50 mo. facility		Diamond - $500,000 Policy Limit $4,500 Home Care Mo. Benefit $6,000 Facility Monthly Benefit 9 years HHC / 7 years facility	
Age	Single	Married	Single	Married	Single	Married	Single	Married
18-29	$14.81	$9.97	$25.75	$17.33	$31.60	$21.27	$36.99	$24.90
30	$15.64	$10.53	$27.16	$18.28	$33.04	$22.24	$39.02	$26.27
31	$16.34	$11.00	$28.57	$19.23	$34.83	$23.45	$41.18	$27.72
32	$17.28	$11.63	$30.10	$20.26	$36.99	$24.90	$43.45	$29.25
33	$18.10	$12.19	$31.74	$21.37	$38.78	$26.11	$45.96	$30.94
34	$19.16	$12.90	$33.51	$22.56	$41.30	$27.80	$48.48	$32.64
35	$20.22	$13.61	$35.39	$23.82	$43.45	$29.25	$51.35	$34.57
36	$21.28	$14.33	$37.39	$25.17	$45.96	$30.94	$54.34	$36.59
37	$22.45	$15.12	$39.50	$26.59	$48.84	$32.88	$57.46	$38.68
38	$23.75	$15.99	$41.85	$28.17	$51.71	$34.81	$60.81	$40.94
39	$25.16	$16.94	$44.20	$29.76	$54.58	$36.75	$64.40	$43.35
40	$26.57	$17.89	$46.91	$31.58	$57.82	$38.92	$68.35	$46.01
41	$28.22	$18.99	$49.73	$33.48	$61.41	$41.34	$72.42	$48.75
42	$29.86	$20.10	$52.67	$35.46	$65.00	$43.76	$76.85	$51.73
43	$31.63	$21.29	$55.84	$37.59	$68.95	$46.41	$81.52	$54.88
44	$33.62	$22.63	$59.37	$39.97	$73.26	$49.32	$86.54	$58.26
45	$35.62	$23.98	$63.01	$42.42	$77.92	$52.46	$91.93	$61.89
46	$37.85	$25.48	$67.01	$45.11	$82.95	$55.84	$97.68	$65.75
47	$40.32	$27.15	$71.36	$48.04	$87.98	$59.23	$103.78	$69.86
48	$42.91	$28.89	$75.95	$51.13	$93.73	$63.10	$110.48	$74.38
49	$45.61	$30.71	$80.88	$54.45	$99.83	$67.21	$117.55	$79.13
50	$48.67	$32.76	$86.17	$58.01	$106.29	$71.56	$125.09	$84.21
51	$51.85	$34.90	$91.82	$61.81	$113.48	$76.39	$133.23	$89.69
52	$55.25	$37.20	$97.93	$65.93	$121.02	$81.47	$141.96	$95.57
53	$58.90	$39.65	$104.51	$70.36	$128.92	$86.79	$151.30	$101.86
54	$62.90	$42.34	$111.57	$75.11	$137.54	$92.59	$161.24	$108.54
55	$67.25	$45.27	$119.21	$80.25	$147.23	$99.12	$172.13	$115.88
56	$72.54	$48.83	$128.73	$86.66	$158.72	$106.85	$185.54	$124.90
57	$77.71	$52.31	$137.66	$92.68	$169.85	$114.35	$198.22	$133.44
58	$83.12	$55.95	$147.42	$99.24	$181.70	$122.32	$211.87	$142.63
59	$89.00	$59.91	$157.89	$106.29	$194.27	$130.78	$226.59	$152.54
60	$95.81	$65.13	$169.88	$115.48	$209.00	$142.08	$243.47	$165.51
61	$103.69	$70.49	$183.87	$124.99	$226.23	$153.79	$263.22	$178.94
62	$111.21	$75.60	$197.27	$134.10	$242.75	$165.02	$282.01	$191.71
63	$120.50	$81.92	$213.73	$145.29	$262.86	$178.69	$305.24	$207.50
64	$130.73	$88.87	$231.83	$157.60	$284.77	$193.58	$330.73	$224.83
65	$142.96	$97.18	$253.82	$172.55	$312.42	$212.38	$362.81	$246.64
66	$156.95	$106.69	$278.74	$189.49	$342.94	$233.13	$398.12	$270.64
67	$169.06	$114.92	$300.25	$204.11	$369.15	$250.95	$428.29	$291.15
68	$181.99	$123.71	$323.18	$219.70	$397.52	$270.24	$460.85	$313.28
69	$195.86	$133.15	$347.87	$236.48	$428.05	$290.99	$495.80	$337.04
70	$210.79	$146.08	$374.79	$256.73	$461.08	$319.53	$533.98	$370.05
71	$231.83	$160.66	$412.29	$285.72	$507.41	$351.63	$587.93	$407.30
72	$249.47	$172.88	$443.92	$307.63	$546.55	$378.76	$632.61	$438.40
73	$268.28	$185.92	$477.42	$330.85	$588.21	$407.63	$680.49	$471.58
74	$288.03	$199.60	$512.69	$355.29	$631.66	$437.74	$730.65	$506.34
75	$369.38	$255.98	$659.29	$456.89	$815.16	$564.90	$945.39	$655.16

* monthly benefit and policy limit amounts do not grow
These rates include "shared waiver" which waives the premium for both spouses when one spouse needs care.

[If you are offering a Partnership plan: "These plans do not qualify for dollar-for dollar asset protection
in the event the insured ever has to apply for Medicaid for applicants under age 76."]

Optional: Insert link to online registration for personal consultations and/or online enrollment.

Customized rates and plans available up to age 85 upon request

Company B
Sample Plans *With* Inflation Coverage (5% Compound No Max)*

Company Logo
Goes Here

Age	Bronze $100 per day 2 years $73,000 initial benefit maximum			Silver $120 per day 2 years $87,600 initial benefit maximum			Gold $130 per day 3 years $142,350 initial benefit maximum			Diamond $150 per day 4 years $219,000 initial benefit maximum		
	Single	Married 1 Issued	Married 2 Issued	Single	Married 1 Issued	Married 2 Issued	Single	Married 1 Issued	Married 2 Issued	Single	Married 1 Issued	Married 2 Issued
18-30	$72.82	$61.32	$49.82	$87.38	$73.58	$59.79	$111.52	$93.91	$76.30	$140.64	$118.44	$96.23
31	$73.48	$61.88	$50.27	$88.17	$74.25	$60.33	$112.53	$94.76	$76.99	$141.92	$119.51	$97.10
32	$74.14	$62.43	$50.73	$88.97	$74.92	$60.87	$113.54	$95.62	$77.69	$143.20	$120.59	$97.98
33	$74.81	$62.99	$51.18	$89.77	$75.59	$61.42	$114.57	$96.48	$78.39	$144.49	$121.68	$98.86
34	$75.48	$63.56	$51.65	$90.58	$76.28	$61.97	$115.60	$97.35	$79.10	$145.80	$122.78	$99.75
35	$76.17	$64.14	$52.11	$91.40	$76.97	$62.54	$116.65	$98.23	$79.81	$147.11	$123.89	$100.66
36	$76.86	$64.72	$52.59	$92.23	$77.67	$63.10	$117.71	$99.12	$80.54	$148.45	$125.01	$101.57
37	$77.55	$65.30	$53.06	$93.06	$78.36	$63.67	$118.76	$100.01	$81.26	$149.78	$126.13	$102.48
38	$78.25	$65.90	$53.54	$93.90	$79.08	$64.25	$119.84	$100.92	$82.00	$151.15	$127.28	$103.42
39	$78.96	$66.49	$54.02	$94.75	$79.79	$64.83	$120.92	$101.83	$82.74	$152.51	$128.43	$104.35
40	$79.67	$67.09	$54.51	$95.60	$80.51	$65.41	$122.02	$102.75	$83.48	$153.88	$129.59	$105.29
41	$80.74	$67.99	$55.24	$96.88	$81.59	$66.29	$123.65	$104.12	$84.60	$155.94	$131.32	$106.70
42	$81.81	$68.90	$55.98	$98.18	$82.68	$67.17	$125.30	$105.52	$85.73	$158.03	$133.08	$108.12
43	$82.90	$69.81	$56.72	$99.48	$83.78	$68.07	$126.97	$106.92	$86.87	$160.13	$134.84	$109.56
44	$84.01	$70.75	$57.48	$100.81	$84.90	$68.98	$128.66	$108.35	$88.03	$162.27	$136.65	$111.03
45	$85.13	$71.69	$58.25	$102.15	$86.02	$69.89	$130.37	$109.79	$89.20	$164.43	$138.46	$112.50
46	$86.27	$72.65	$59.02	$103.52	$87.18	$70.83	$132.12	$111.26	$90.40	$166.62	$140.32	$114.01
47	$87.42	$73.62	$59.81	$104.90	$88.34	$71.78	$133.88	$112.74	$91.61	$168.85	$142.19	$115.53
48	$88.58	$74.59	$60.61	$106.30	$89.51	$72.73	$135.66	$114.24	$92.82	$171.09	$144.08	$117.06
49	$89.76	$75.59	$61.42	$107.72	$90.71	$73.70	$137.47	$115.77	$94.06	$173.38	$146.00	$118.63
50	$90.96	$76.60	$62.24	$109.15	$91.92	$74.68	$139.31	$117.31	$95.32	$175.69	$147.95	$120.21
51	$94.13	$79.27	$64.41	$112.96	$95.13	$77.29	$144.17	$121.40	$98.64	$181.82	$153.11	$124.40
52	$97.42	$82.04	$66.65	$116.90	$98.44	$79.99	$149.20	$125.64	$102.08	$188.16	$158.45	$128.74
53	$100.82	$84.90	$68.98	$120.98	$101.88	$82.78	$154.41	$130.03	$105.65	$194.73	$163.99	$133.24
54	$104.33	$87.86	$71.38	$125.20	$105.43	$85.66	$159.78	$134.56	$109.33	$201.52	$169.70	$137.88
55	$107.97	$90.93	$73.88	$129.57	$109.11	$88.65	$165.36	$139.25	$113.14	$208.55	$175.62	$142.69
56	$111.74	$94.09	$76.45	$134.08	$112.91	$91.74	$171.12	$144.11	$117.09	$215.82	$181.74	$147.67
57	$115.64	$97.38	$79.12	$138.76	$116.85	$94.94	$177.10	$149.14	$121.17	$223.35	$188.09	$152.82
58	$119.67	$100.77	$81.88	$143.60	$120.93	$98.26	$183.28	$154.34	$125.40	$231.14	$194.65	$158.15
59	$123.84	$104.29	$84.73	$148.61	$125.15	$101.68	$189.67	$159.72	$129.77	$239.20	$201.43	$163.67
60	$128.16	$107.93	$87.69	$153.80	$129.51	$105.23	$196.28	$165.29	$134.30	$247.55	$208.46	$169.37
61	$135.74	$114.30	$92.87	$162.88	$137.17	$111.45	$207.88	$175.06	$142.23	$262.18	$220.78	$179.38
62	$143.76	$121.06	$98.36	$172.51	$145.27	$118.03	$220.17	$185.40	$150.64	$277.67	$233.83	$189.99
63	$152.25	$128.21	$104.17	$182.70	$153.85	$125.01	$233.17	$196.36	$159.54	$294.07	$247.64	$201.21
64	$161.25	$135.79	$110.33	$193.50	$162.95	$132.39	$246.96	$207.96	$168.97	$311.46	$262.28	$213.10
65	$170.78	$143.81	$116.85	$204.93	$172.58	$140.22	$261.55	$220.25	$178.95	$329.86	$277.78	$225.69
66	$185.32	$156.06	$126.80	$222.38	$187.27	$152.15	$283.81	$239.00	$194.19	$357.94	$301.42	$244.91
67	$201.10	$169.35	$137.60	$241.32	$203.22	$165.12	$307.99	$259.36	$210.73	$388.43	$327.10	$265.77
68	$218.23	$183.77	$149.31	$261.87	$220.53	$179.18	$334.22	$281.45	$228.68	$421.51	$354.95	$288.40
69	$236.81	$199.42	$162.03	$284.18	$239.31	$194.44	$362.68	$305.42	$248.15	$457.41	$385.18	$312.96
70	$256.98	$216.40	$175.83	$308.37	$259.68	$210.99	$393.57	$331.42	$269.28	$496.36	$417.98	$339.61
71	$282.89	$238.22	$193.56	$339.47	$285.87	$232.27	$433.25	$364.84	$296.43	$546.40	$460.13	$373.85
72	$311.41	$262.24	$213.07	$373.70	$314.69	$255.69	$476.93	$401.63	$326.32	$601.50	$506.53	$411.55
73	$342.81	$288.68	$234.56	$411.38	$346.42	$281.47	$525.02	$442.12	$359.22	$662.14	$557.60	$453.05
74	$377.38	$317.79	$258.20	$452.85	$381.35	$309.85	$577.96	$486.70	$395.44	$728.91	$613.82	$498.72
75	$415.43	$349.84	$284.24	$498.52	$419.80	$341.09	$636.23	$535.78	$435.32	$802.41	$675.71	$549.01
76	$454.69	$382.90	$311.10	$545.63	$459.47	$373.32	$696.36	$586.41	$476.46	$878.23	$739.57	$600.90
77	$497.66	$419.08	$340.50	$597.19	$502.90	$408.60	$762.16	$641.82	$521.48	$961.23	$809.45	$657.68
78	$544.68	$458.68	$372.68	$653.62	$550.41	$447.21	$834.18	$702.47	$570.76	$1,052.05	$885.94	$719.83
79	$596.15	$502.03	$407.90	$715.39	$602.43	$489.47	$913.02	$768.86	$624.70	$1,151.48	$969.67	$787.85

* all monthly and policy limits grow 5% compounded annually, as long as benefits are not exhausted.

[*If you are offering a Partnership plan:* "These plans qualify for dollar-for-dollar asset protection in the event the insured ever has to apply for Medicaid."]

Optional: Insert link to online registration for personal consultations and/or online enrollment.

Company B
Sample Plans _Without_ Inflation Coverage*

Company Logo
Goes Here

	Bronze	Silver	Gold	Diamond
	$100 per day	$120 per day	$130 per day	$150 per day
	2 years	2 years	3 years	4 years
	$73,000 benefit maximum	$87,600 benefit maximum	$142,350 benefit maximum	$219,000 benefit maximum

Age	Single	Married 1 Issued	Married 2 Issued	Single	Married 1 Issued	Married 2 Issued	Single	Married 1 Issued	Married 2 Issued	Single	Married 1 Issued	Married 2 Issued
18-30	$31.21	$26.28	$21.35	$37.45	$31.54	$25.62	$47.79	$40.25	$32.70	$60.28	$50.76	$41.24
31	$31.53	$26.55	$21.57	$37.84	$31.86	$25.89	$48.29	$40.66	$33.04	$60.90	$51.28	$41.67
32	$31.86	$26.83	$21.80	$38.23	$32.20	$26.16	$48.79	$41.09	$33.39	$61.54	$51.82	$42.11
33	$32.20	$27.11	$22.03	$38.64	$32.54	$26.44	$49.31	$41.53	$33.74	$62.19	$52.37	$42.55
34	$32.54	$27.40	$22.26	$39.04	$32.88	$26.71	$49.83	$41.96	$34.09	$62.85	$52.92	$43.00
35	$32.88	$27.69	$22.50	$39.46	$33.23	$27.00	$50.36	$42.41	$34.46	$63.51	$53.48	$43.45
36	$33.23	$27.98	$22.73	$39.87	$33.58	$27.28	$50.89	$42.85	$34.82	$64.18	$54.04	$43.91
37	$33.57	$28.27	$22.97	$40.29	$33.93	$27.56	$51.42	$43.30	$35.18	$64.84	$54.61	$44.37
38	$33.93	$28.57	$23.22	$40.72	$34.29	$27.86	$51.97	$43.76	$35.56	$65.54	$55.19	$44.84
39	$34.28	$28.87	$23.46	$41.14	$34.65	$28.15	$52.51	$44.22	$35.93	$66.22	$55.77	$45.31
40	$34.65	$29.18	$23.70	$41.57	$35.01	$28.45	$53.06	$44.68	$36.30	$66.92	$56.35	$45.79
41	$35.17	$29.61	$24.06	$42.20	$35.54	$28.87	$53.86	$45.35	$36.85	$67.92	$57.20	$46.47
42	$35.69	$30.05	$24.42	$42.83	$36.06	$29.30	$54.66	$46.03	$37.40	$68.93	$58.05	$47.16
43	$36.22	$30.50	$24.78	$43.46	$36.60	$29.74	$55.47	$46.71	$37.95	$69.95	$58.91	$47.86
44	$36.76	$30.96	$25.15	$44.11	$37.15	$30.18	$56.30	$47.41	$38.52	$71.00	$59.79	$48.58
45	$37.31	$31.42	$25.53	$44.77	$37.70	$30.64	$57.14	$48.12	$39.10	$72.07	$60.69	$49.31
46	$37.86	$31.88	$25.91	$45.43	$38.26	$31.09	$57.99	$48.83	$39.67	$73.13	$61.59	$50.04
47	$38.43	$32.36	$26.29	$46.11	$38.83	$31.55	$58.85	$49.56	$40.27	$74.22	$62.50	$50.78
48	$39.00	$32.84	$26.69	$46.80	$39.41	$32.02	$59.73	$50.30	$40.87	$75.33	$63.44	$51.54
49	$39.58	$33.33	$27.08	$47.50	$40.00	$32.50	$60.62	$51.05	$41.48	$76.45	$64.38	$52.31
50	$40.18	$33.83	$27.49	$48.21	$40.60	$32.99	$61.53	$51.81	$42.10	$77.60	$65.35	$53.10
51	$42.09	$35.44	$28.80	$50.50	$42.53	$34.56	$64.46	$54.28	$44.10	$81.29	$68.46	$55.62
52	$44.08	$37.12	$30.16	$52.90	$44.55	$36.20	$67.52	$56.86	$46.20	$85.15	$71.70	$58.26
53	$46.18	$38.89	$31.60	$55.41	$46.66	$37.92	$70.72	$59.56	$48.39	$89.19	$75.11	$61.03
54	$48.37	$40.74	$33.10	$58.05	$48.88	$39.72	$74.09	$62.39	$50.69	$93.44	$78.68	$63.93
55	$50.67	$42.67	$34.67	$60.80	$51.20	$41.60	$77.60	$65.34	$53.09	$97.86	$82.41	$66.96
56	$53.08	$44.70	$36.32	$63.69	$53.64	$43.58	$81.29	$68.45	$55.62	$102.52	$86.33	$70.14
57	$55.60	$46.82	$38.04	$66.71	$56.18	$45.65	$85.15	$71.70	$58.26	$107.38	$90.43	$73.47
58	$58.24	$49.04	$39.85	$69.89	$58.85	$47.82	$89.20	$75.11	$61.03	$112.49	$94.73	$76.97
59	$61.01	$51.38	$41.74	$73.21	$61.65	$50.09	$93.44	$78.68	$63.93	$117.84	$99.24	$80.63
60	$63.91	$53.81	$43.72	$76.69	$64.58	$52.47	$97.87	$82.42	$66.96	$123.43	$103.94	$84.45
61	$68.99	$58.10	$47.20	$82.79	$69.71	$56.64	$105.66	$88.97	$72.29	$133.25	$112.21	$91.17
62	$74.48	$62.72	$50.96	$89.38	$75.27	$61.16	$114.07	$96.06	$78.05	$143.87	$121.15	$98.44
63	$80.40	$67.71	$55.01	$96.49	$81.25	$66.02	$123.14	$103.70	$84.25	$155.30	$130.78	$106.26
64	$86.80	$73.10	$59.39	$104.16	$87.72	$71.27	$132.94	$111.95	$90.96	$167.66	$141.19	$114.71
65	$93.72	$78.92	$64.12	$112.46	$94.70	$76.95	$143.53	$120.86	$98.20	$181.01	$152.43	$123.85
66	$103.86	$87.46	$71.06	$124.63	$104.95	$85.28	$159.06	$133.95	$108.83	$200.61	$168.93	$137.26
67	$115.11	$96.93	$78.76	$138.13	$116.32	$94.51	$176.29	$148.45	$120.62	$222.33	$187.23	$152.12
68	$127.58	$107.43	$87.29	$153.09	$128.92	$104.75	$195.38	$164.53	$133.68	$246.41	$207.50	$168.60
69	$141.39	$119.07	$96.74	$169.67	$142.88	$116.09	$216.54	$182.35	$148.16	$273.10	$229.98	$186.86
70	$156.70	$131.96	$107.22	$188.04	$158.35	$128.66	$239.99	$202.10	$164.20	$302.67	$254.88	$207.09
71	$175.72	$147.97	$120.23	$210.86	$177.56	$144.27	$269.11	$226.62	$184.13	$339.39	$285.81	$232.22
72	$197.03	$165.92	$134.81	$236.43	$199.10	$161.77	$301.75	$254.10	$206.46	$380.56	$320.47	$260.38
73	$220.92	$186.04	$151.16	$265.11	$223.25	$181.39	$338.35	$284.92	$231.50	$426.72	$359.34	$291.96
74	$247.72	$208.60	$169.49	$297.26	$250.32	$203.39	$379.38	$319.48	$259.57	$478.46	$402.92	$327.37
75	$277.76	$233.90	$190.05	$333.31	$280.69	$228.06	$425.39	$358.23	$291.06	$536.50	$451.79	$367.08
76	$308.59	$259.86	$211.14	$370.30	$311.83	$253.37	$472.60	$397.98	$323.36	$596.04	$501.92	$407.81
77	$342.83	$288.70	$234.57	$411.39	$346.44	$281.48	$525.04	$442.14	$359.24	$662.17	$557.62	$453.07
78	$380.87	$320.73	$260.59	$457.04	$384.88	$312.71	$583.30	$491.20	$399.10	$735.65	$619.49	$503.34
79	$423.12	$356.31	$289.50	$507.75	$427.58	$347.41	$648.01	$545.70	$443.38	$817.26	$688.22	$559.18

*Daily benefit and policy limit amounts do not grow.

[If you are offering a Partnership plan: *For applicants under age 76, these plans do not qualify for dollar-for dollar asset protection in the event the insured ever has to apply for Medicaid.*]

Optional: Insert link to online registration for personal consultations and/or online enrollment.

Company C
Sample Plans With Inflation Coverage (5% Compound No Max)*

Company Logo
Goes Here

Age	Bronze - $73,000 Initial Policy Max $100 Initial Daily Benefit 2 years ($100 X 730 days)	Silver - $109,500 Initial Policy Limit $150 Initial Daily Benefit 2 years ($150 x 730 days)	Gold - $219,000 Initial Policy Max $150 Initial Daily Benefit 4 years ($150 x 1,460 days)	Diamond - $292,000 Initial Policy Max $200 Initial Daily Benefit 4 years ($200 x 1,460 days)
29	$39.00	$58.50	$83.40	$111.20
30	$39.00	$58.50	$83.40	$111.20
31	$39.60	$59.40	$84.90	$113.20
32	$40.20	$60.30	$86.40	$115.20
33	$41.00	$61.50	$88.20	$117.60
34	$41.60	$62.40	$89.70	$119.60
35	$42.20	$63.30	$91.50	$122.00
36	$43.00	$64.50	$93.00	$124.00
37	$43.60	$65.40	$94.80	$126.40
38	$44.40	$66.60	$96.60	$128.80
39	$45.20	$67.80	$98.40	$131.20
40	$45.80	$68.70	$100.20	$133.60
41	$46.40	$69.60	$102.00	$136.00
42	$47.00	$70.50	$104.10	$138.80
43	$47.60	$71.40	$106.20	$141.60
44	$48.20	$72.30	$108.30	$144.40
45	$48.80	$73.20	$110.40	$147.20
46	$49.60	$74.40	$112.20	$149.60
47	$50.40	$75.60	$114.30	$152.40
48	$51.00	$76.50	$116.40	$155.20
49	$51.80	$77.70	$118.80	$158.40
50	$52.60	$78.90	$120.90	$161.20
51	$54.40	$81.60	$124.50	$166.00
52	$56.00	$84.00	$128.10	$170.80
53	$57.80	$86.70	$131.70	$175.60
54	$59.80	$89.70	$135.60	$180.80
55	$61.60	$92.40	$139.50	$186.00
56	$63.60	$95.40	$144.30	$192.40
57	$65.60	$98.40	$149.40	$199.20
58	$67.80	$101.70	$154.50	$206.00
59	$70.00	$105.00	$159.90	$213.20
60	$72.20	$108.30	$165.60	$220.80
61	$77.20	$115.80	$175.20	$233.60
62	$82.40	$123.60	$185.70	$247.60
63	$88.00	$132.00	$196.50	$262.00
64	$93.80	$140.70	$207.90	$277.20
65	$100.20	$150.30	$220.20	$293.60
66	$106.00	$159.00	$234.00	$312.00
67	$112.20	$168.30	$248.40	$331.20
68	$118.80	$178.20	$264.00	$352.00
69	$125.80	$188.70	$280.50	$374.00
70	$133.00	$199.50	$297.90	$397.20
71	$146.40	$219.60	$331.20	$441.60
72	$161.00	$241.50	$368.40	$491.20
73	$177.20	$265.80	$409.80	$546.40
74	$194.80	$292.20	$455.70	$607.60
75	$214.40	$321.60	$506.70	$675.60

monthly and policy limits grow 5% compounded annually, as long as benefits are not exhausted.
u are offering a Partnership plan: These plans qualify for dollar-for-dollar asset protection in the event the insured ever has to apply for Medicaid]
nal: Insert link to online registration for personal consultations and/or online enrollment.

Customized rates and plans available up to age 84 upon request

Company C
Sample Plans with Future Purchase Inflation Offers*

Company Logo
Goes Here

Age	Bronze - $73,000 Policy Limit $100 Daily Benefit 2 years ($100 X 730 days)	Silver - $109,500 Policy Limit $150 Daily Benefit 2 years ($150 x 730 days)	Gold - $219,000 Policy Limit $150 Daily Benefit 4 years ($150 x 1,460 days)	Diamond - $292,000 Policy Limit $200 Daily Benefit 4 years ($200 x 1,460 days)
18-29	$16.20	$24.30	$35.10	$46.80
30	$16.20	$24.30	$35.10	$46.80
31	$16.40	$24.60	$35.40	$47.20
32	$16.40	$24.60	$36.00	$48.00
33	$16.60	$24.90	$36.60	$48.80
34	$16.80	$25.20	$36.90	$49.20
35	$17.00	$25.50	$37.50	$50.00
36	$17.20	$25.80	$38.10	$50.80
37	$17.40	$26.10	$38.40	$51.20
38	$17.60	$26.40	$39.00	$52.00
39	$17.80	$26.70	$39.60	$52.80
40	$18.00	$27.00	$40.20	$53.60
41	$18.40	$27.60	$41.10	$54.80
42	$18.80	$28.20	$42.00	$56.00
43	$19.40	$29.10	$42.90	$57.20
44	$19.80	$29.70	$43.80	$58.40
45	$20.20	$30.30	$45.00	$60.00
46	$20.60	$30.90	$45.60	$60.80
47	$21.00	$31.50	$46.50	$62.00
48	$21.60	$32.40	$47.40	$63.20
49	$22.00	$33.00	$48.30	$64.40
50	$22.40	$33.60	$49.20	$65.60
51	$23.00	$34.50	$50.40	$67.20
52	$23.60	$35.40	$51.90	$69.20
53	$24.20	$36.30	$53.40	$71.20
54	$24.80	$37.20	$54.90	$73.20
55	$25.60	$38.40	$56.40	$75.20
56	$27.80	$41.70	$60.00	$80.00
57	$30.20	$45.30	$63.90	$85.20
58	$32.80	$49.20	$68.40	$91.20
59	$35.60	$53.40	$72.90	$97.20
60	$38.60	$57.90	$77.70	$103.60
61	$41.40	$62.10	$83.70	$111.60
62	$44.40	$66.60	$90.00	$120.00
63	$47.60	$71.40	$97.20	$129.60
64	$51.20	$76.80	$104.70	$139.60
65	$55.00	$82.50	$112.80	$150.40
66	$59.60	$89.40	$123.00	$164.00
67	$64.40	$96.60	$133.80	$178.40
68	$69.80	$104.70	$145.80	$194.40
69	$75.80	$113.70	$158.70	$211.60
70	$82.00	$123.00	$172.80	$230.40
71	$92.20	$138.30	$194.10	$258.80
72	$103.60	$155.40	$218.10	$290.80
73	$116.60	$174.90	$244.80	$326.40
74	$131.00	$196.50	$275.10	$366.80
75	$147.20	$220.80	$309.00	$412.00

* **offer to increase daily benefit and policy limit every three years at attained age premium with no health questions**
[*Customize this message for your state if you are offering a Partnership plan, as a few states do allow FPO/GPO for younger ages:* "For applicants under age 76, these plans do not qualify for dollar-for-dollar asset protection in the event the insured ever has to apply for Medicaid."]
Optional: Insert link to online registration for personal consultations and/or online enrollment.
Customized rates and plans available up to age 84 upon request

SAMPLE ENROLLMENT INSTRUCTIONS FOR EMPLOYEES AND FAMILY MEMBERS

Let's drill down to the basic instructions for enrollment.

These instructions are for a plan with simplified underwriting for working spouses and online enrollment for all applicants. Notice that I positioned the online instructions first to encourage online enrollment. You should customize the instructions to each case. These are merely to demonstrate the level of detail I have used and get you started in the right direction if you decide to use written enrollment instructions.

<u>Instructions for Completing SIMPLIFIED OnLine Application</u>
<u>for Long-Term Care Insurance:</u>
EMPLOYEES AND SPOUSES WHO WORK 30+ HOURS PER WEEK

Important: Each applicant must complete his or her own online application by [date].

Go to [URL for insurance company]

Select your state of residence.

Click on "Start a New Application".

Complete your personal information. Indicate if you the employee or the spouse/care partner. Spouses/care partners must enter the employee's name and Social Security # to establish eligibility for this plan. A spouse will be asked to type in the name of the spouse's employer and phone number as the spouse's employment will be verified to establish eligibility for the limited health questions.

Answer the rest of the questions, using the paper application instructions below for help if you need it. Use the benefit descriptions below to select your benefits, or you may select other benefits by using the rate calculator. At the end of the application, you will have an opportunity to save and print a copy for yourself. You will then have an opportunity to start a new application for your spouse or other family member.

Questions? Call [your agency name] at 800-XXX-XXX or email name@xxxxx.com

[Name of Insurance Company] Customer Service can also help with your online application at (800) XXX-XXXX between the hours of [insert times].

Instructions for Completing SIMPLIFIED Paper Application
MUST COMPLETE BY [date]
(Give completed applications to [HR Department] or bring to your personal consultation. Sign up for a personal consultation at [link to personal consultations])
Important: Employees and spouses must fill out separate applications
(Example – employee and spouse = 2 applications)

Page 1 - Health Questions: Print your name and Social Security # at top of page. Answer the six health questions and **sign and date** at the bottom. (If "yes" to any of the first three, please do not submit an application.)

Page 2 – HIPAA Medical Authorization: Print name, date of birth, SS# and sign and date at the bottom.

Section I, Applicant Information:

#1   Complete personal information.

#2-A Employees check this box as the employee

#2-B Spouses or partners* who work 30+ hours a week anywhere check the box that says "Care Partner" and write the employee's name and Social Security #.

#3   Check the box that says "I meet the definition of Actively-At-Work".

Working spouses should enter employer's name and phone number or mark self-employed. (This information entitles a working spouse to enroll with a limited number of health questions.)

#4   Answer question about spouse or partner applying. **Please note that single applicants with a care partner must complete the separate care partner statement later in the application whether or not both are applying.**

*Care partner means anyone who has been in a single dedicated relationship of at least 12 months while sharing the same residence and not being related by blood.

#5-7 Complete these, skipping #5 if your spouse/partner is not applying.

Section II, Insurance History:

Complete item 1 by checking "no" that you are not covered by Medicaid. Answer the questions about having another long-term care insurance policy.
Important: You do not have to replace an older policy to have this policy.

Section III, Policy Benefit Selection, and make one of these selections:

<u>Bronze Plan</u>
Cash Benefit Account: $100,000
Monthly Cash Benefit - $3,000 and Enhanced Facility Benefit (EFB) $4,000

<u>Silver Plan</u>
Cash Benefit Account: $200,000
Monthly Cash Benefit - $4,500 and Enhanced Facility Benefit (EFB) $6,000

<u>Gold Plan</u>
Cash Benefit Account: $300,000
Monthly Cash Benefit - $4,500 and Enhanced Facility Benefit (EFB) $6,000

<u>Diamond Plan</u>
Cash Benefit Account: $500,000
Monthly Cash Benefit - $4,500 and Enhanced Facility Benefit (EFB) $6,000

<u>All Plans</u>
Elimination Period - 90 days
Inflation/Benefit Increase Rider: Indicate your inflation decision as either

163

"5% Compound 2X Max" or "none"
Premium Payment Options: Lifetime
Riders: Check "yes" only for Shared Waiver of Premium Rider if your spouse is also enrolling

Rates for other benefit options and payment intervals are available at the [name of insurance company] website by following the instructions above for online enrollment.

Section IV. Premium Payment Information

Check #5, Payroll Deduction, sign your name, and insert your Social Security number (unless you prefer to pay quarterly, semi-annually or annually for up to a 9% premium savings). IMPORTANT: The active employee must sign this form on the spouse's application for a spouse's premium to be payroll deducted.

Section V. Signatures and Authorizations

#1 - Everyone must complete this section.
#2 - indicate if you want another individual notified if you don't pay your premium (this
    is for your protection in the event you are not able to pay your premium due to a
    physical or cognitive disorder)
#3 - indicate if you accept or reject inflation coverage
#4 - check that you "reject" the shortened benefit period rider
#5 - sign and date

Section VI. Producer's Statement – SKIP THIS SECTION

Replacement Forms: Skip these unless you are replacing an older long-term care insurance policy. Only sign the forms if you are replacing a policy (you may keep one of these forms). Remember, you don't have to replace an older LTC insurance policy. You can have this one in addition to the older policy.

Care Partner Statement – SKIP THIS FORM IF YOU ARE SINGLE WITHOUT A CARE PARTNER OR MARRIED

Long-Term Care Insurance Personal Worksheet

Complete by either answering the questions about assets and income or checking that you do not wish to complete the information. Regardless of your decision, you must SIGN YOUR NAME BELOW THE BOX THAT INDICATES YOUR DECISION.

If you do not wish to disclose financial information, you must also sign the "Authorization Form for Financial Non-Disclosure on the Long-Term Care Insurance Personal Worksheet" on the next page. You may keep the Outline of Coverage at the back of the application.

You may keep the Outline of Coverage at the back of the application until you receive your policy (certificate).

Questions? Call [your agency name] at 800-XXX-XXX or email name@xxxxx.com

<u>Instructions for Completing MODIFIED Online Application</u>
<u>for Long-Term Care Insurance for Non-Working Spouses or Spouses Who Work LESS</u>
<u>THAN 30 HOURS PER WEEK or Other Eligible Family Members (parents, grandparents,</u>
<u>siblings, adult children 18+)</u>

Important: Each applicant must complete his or her own online application.

Go to [URL for insurance company]

Select your state of residence.

Click on "Start a New Application".

Complete your personal information. Check your relationship to the employee and enter the employee's name and Social Security #. A non-working spouse would check the box that says "Care Partner", and then would check the box that says "I do not meet the definition of Actively-At-Work".

Answer the rest of the questions, using the paper application instructions below for help if you need it. Use the benefit descriptions below to select your benefits, or you may select other benefits by using the rate calculator. At the end of the application, you will have an opportunity to save and print a copy for yourself. You will then have an opportunity to start a new application for another family member.

Questions? Call [your company name] at 800-XXX-XXX or email name@xxxxx.com

[Name of Insurance Company] Customer Service can also help with your online application at (800) XXX-XXXX between the hours of [insert times].

Instructions for Completing MODIFIED Paper Application

Give completed applications to [HR Department] or bring to your personal consultation. Sign up for a personal consultation at [link to personal consultations]. Spouses and family members are welcome at these consultations.

Important: All applicants must fill out an application (Example: employee, spouse, mother-in-law and adult child = 4 applications)

Page 1 - Health Questions: Print your name and Social Security # at top of page. Answer the six health questions and **sign and date** at the bottom. (If "yes" to any of the first three, please do not submit an application.)

Page 2 – Health Questions (cont.) List all prescription medications or mark "No Medications". List physicians who have treated you in the past 5 years and **sign and date** at the bottom.

Page 3 - HIPAA Medical Authorization: Print name, date of birth, SS# and sign and date at the bottom.

Section I, Applicant Information:
#1 Complete personal information.
#2-B Check your relationship to the [employer's name] employee and enter the employee's name and Social Security #. A non-working spouse would check the box that says "Care Partner" #3B Check the box that says "I do not meet the definition of Actively-At-Work".
#4 Answer question about spouse or partner applying. **Please note that single applicants with a care partner must complete the separate care partner statement later in the application whether or not you both are applying.**

*Care partner means anyone who has been in a single dedicated relationship of at least 12 months while sharing the same residence and not being related by blood.

#5-7 Complete these, skipping #5 if your spouse/partner is not applying.

Section II, Insurance History:

Complete item 1 by checking "no" that you are not covered by Medicaid. Answer the questions about having another long-term care insurance policy.
Important: You do not have to replace an older policy to have this policy.

Section III, Policy Benefit Selection, and make one of these selections:

Bronze Plan
Cash Benefit Account: $100,000
Monthly Cash Benefit - $3,000 and Enhanced Facility Benefit (EFB) $4,000

Silver Plan
Cash Benefit Account: $200,000
Monthly Cash Benefit - $4,500 and Enhanced Facility Benefit (EFB) $6,000

Gold Plan
Cash Benefit Account: $300,000
Monthly Cash Benefit - $4,500 and Enhanced Facility Benefit (EFB) $6,000

Diamond Plan
Cash Benefit Account: $500,000
Monthly Cash Benefit - $4,500 and Enhanced Facility Benefit (EFB) $6,000

All Plans
Elimination Period - 90 days
Inflation/Benefit Increase Rider: Indicate your inflation decision as either "5% Compound 2X Max" or "none"

Premium Payment Options: Lifetime
Riders: Check "yes" only for Shared Waiver of Premium Rider if your spouse is also enrolling

Rates for other benefit options and payment intervals are available at the [Name of Insurance Company] website by following the instructions above for online enrollment.

Section IV. Premium Payment Information

> Check #5, Payroll Deduction, sign your name, and insert your Social Security number (unless you prefer to pay quarterly, semi-annually or annually for up to a 9% premium savings). **IMPORTANT: The active employee must sign this form on the spouse's application for a spouse's premium to be payroll deducted.**

Section V. Signatures and Authorizations

#1 - Everyone must complete this section.
#2 – indicate if you want another individual notified if you don't pay your premium (this is for your protection in the event you are not able to pay your premium due to a physical or cognitive disorder)
#3 – indicate if you accept or reject inflation coverage
#4 – check that you "reject" the shortened benefit period rider
#5 – sign and date

Section VI. Producer's Statement – SKIP THIS SECTION

Replacement Forms: Skip these unless you are replacing an older long-term care insurance policy. Only sign the forms if you are replacing a policy (you may keep one of these forms). Remember, you don't have to replace an older LTC insurance policy. You can have this one in addition to the older policy.

Care Partner Statement – SKIP THIS FORM IF YOU ARE SINGLE WITHOUT A CARE PARTNER OR MARRIED

Long-Term Care Insurance Personal Worksheet

> Complete by either answering the questions about assets and income or checking that you do not wish to complete the information. Regardless of your decision, you must SIGN YOUR NAME BELOW THE BOX THAT INDICATES YOUR DECISION.

> If you do not wish to disclose financial information, you must also sign the "Authorization Form for Financial Non-Disclosure on the Long-Term Care Insurance Personal Worksheet" on the next page.

You may keep the Outline of Coverage at the back of the application until you receive your policy (certificate).

Questions? Call [your agency name] at 800-XXX-XXX or email name@xxxxx.com

167